P9-DGJ-527

A Reference Publication in Literature
Ronald Gottesman, *Editor*

Henry Adams:
A Reference Guide

Earl N. Harbert

G. K. HALL & CO., 70 LINCOLN STREET, BOSTON, MASS.

LIBRARY OF CONGRESS CATALOGING IN PUBLICATION DATA

Harbert, Earl N. 1934-
Henry Adams: a reference guide.

(Reference publications in literature)
Includes index.
1. Adams, Henry, 1838-1918--Bibliography
I. Series.
Z8015.3.A21 Suppl [E175.5] 016.973'07'20924
ISBN 0-8161-7975-1 77-13492

This publication is printed on permanent/durable acid-free paper
MANUFACTURED IN THE UNITED STATES OF AMERICA

Contents

Introduction

The modern reputation of Henry Adams dates from 1918, the year that marked both the death of the less-than-well-known author and the first general publication of a book that has since become an acknowledged American classic--*The Education of Henry Adams*. As this *Reference Guide* documents, before that year Adams's writings had brought him to the attention of only a small number of serious critics and reviewers, who associated his name with the historical efforts represented by the nine-volume *History of the United States During the Administrations of Thomas Jefferson and James Madison* (1889-1891) and *Mont-Saint-Michel and Chartres* (1913). His fictional works were practically unremembered and unknown, largely because the secret of their authorship was closely kept.

In 1918, *The Education of Henry Adams* burst upon this quiet horizon, first to make Henry Adams a posthumous best-selling author and then to open the way for the critical reconsideration of the whole body of Adams's writings which still continues. Yet even now, almost sixty years after Adams's death and since the *Education* made its mark, readers are still without a collected edition of Henry Adams's writings. In fact, only as recently as 1973 did a reliable text of the *Education* become available to the general public (*See* 1973.B8), and we are still awaiting the appearance of his collected letters, although editorial work on the project is reported well underway.

By any fair measure, the critical fate of Henry Adams has been mixed, a combination of close attention to the details of his life and thought and to certain of his titles with a curious and almost cavalier disregard for the larger scope and variety of his life's work in the forms of essays, biographies, poetry, and personal correspondence.

Not surprisingly, *The Education of Henry Adams*, more than any other single achievement, cast the shadow that has defined most of the commentary and criticism on its author. Early reviewers such as Paul Elmer More, writing in *The Unpartizan Review*, fixed upon "the baffled sense of mystery" surrounding Adams's account of his life. That "mystery" led T. S. Eliot, in the pages of the *Athenaeum*, to express his doubts about the adequacy of the subtitle "An Autobiography" as a description of the *Education*. From 1918 until 1964, the biographical questions raised by that book persistently dominated most of the serious consideration of Henry Adams. In articles and, even more, in a series of biographical volumes, including collections of Adams's letters, two generations of scholars managed to clear away much of the "mystery" about the man, so that other critics could concentrate their attention on his writings. Milestones on this path were: four volumes of letters, published as *A Cycle of Adams Letters* and *Letters of Henry Adams*, edited by Worthington C. Ford; *Henry Adams and His Friends: A Collection of His Unpublished Letters*, edited and introduced by Harold Dean Cater; two ambitious biographies, *The Adams Family* and *Henry Adams*, written by James Truslow Adams (himself not a member of the family); Elizabeth Stevenson's *Henry Adams: A Biography*; and, perhaps most important of all, the three-volume biography, written by Ernest Samuels, that has established itself as a standard reference work: *The Young Henry Adams*, *Henry Adams: The Middle Years*, and *Henry Adams: The Major Phase*. An appendix to each volume contains a chronological listing of "The Writings of Henry Adams."

The appearance of Henry Holt's *Garrulities of an Octogenarian Editor*, in 1923, confirmed the facts of Adams's authorship of two novels, *Democracy* and *Esther*, and opened the way for various considerations of the novelist's ideas on politics, literature, and religion. Morris Speare's *The Political Novel: Its Development in England and America* (1924) represents a pioneering effort in this direction, which R. P. Blackmur and Robert E. Spiller explored to great advantage in many essays, introductions, and chapters in books. Some of the rich possibilities of Adams's two novels may be fairly sampled in the discussions of C. Vann Woodward, *The Burden of Southern History*, and Millicent Bell, "Adams' Esther: The Morality of Taste," which appeared in the *New England Quarterly* in 1962. Overall, commentary on Adams the novelist has added impressive evidence to the case for his reputation as a man of letters, whose literary achievements must be judged larger than those of a historian alone.

Yet, as early as 1927, Henry Steele Commager, writing in the *South Atlantic Quarterly*, pronounced the *History of the Administrations of Thomas Jefferson and James Madison* "definitive" and *Mont-Saint-Michel and Chartres* "the most perfect thing Henry Adams ever wrote." Such judgments have more recently given way to a closer examination of the artistic technique in both books, such as the studies of *Chartres* by John J. Conder, *A Formula of His Own: Henry Adams's Literary Experiment* and Robert Mane's *Henry Adams on the Road to Chartres*; and a comparative analysis of the *History* by Richard C. Vitzthum, *The American Compromise: Theme and Method in the Histories of Bancroft, Parkman, and Adams*. Along the way, the complex questions of "scientific history" and of Henry Adams as historiographer have often been introduced and considered, most fully perhaps in William Jordy's *Henry Adams: Scientific Historian*.

Introduction

For the reader who prefers a more general introduction to the life and writings of Henry Adams, the last sixty years have provided abundant resources. A mixture of biographical and literary discussion may be found in Robert E. Spiller's chapter "Henry Adams" in the *Literary History of the United States* and in Ernest Samuels's remarks on Adams in the two-volume anthology, *Major Writers of America*, edited by Perry Miller. A more detailed consideration, George Hochfield's *Henry Adams: An Introduction and Interpretation*, is generally available in bookstores and libraries; it surveys the basic problems raised by Adams's work. For advanced readers, J. C. Levenson's *Mind and Art of Henry Adams* provides a useful synthesis of biographical facts and interpretations of Adams's thought and writing. Although this book first appeared in 1957, it has aged gracefully and still holds its place as a standard critical reference. Even more fundamental to the task of interpreting what Adams meant is a broad familiarity with his works, a list of which may be found in the following section of this *Reference Guide*: "Major Writings by Henry Adams."

I have compiled this *Reference Guide* with the intent of providing a usable pathway through the bewildering tangle of diverse and conflicting opinions surrounding Henry Adams. Yet, I have tried to keep in mind at all times the special richness and variety of the available commentary, and to represent those important qualities in both selections and annotations. As it now appears in print, this volume is intentionally selective; within the limits of a "Guide" it would simply not be possible to include all of the published references to Henry Adams that appeared from 1879 to the end of 1975. Thus, among the profusion of reviews, brief notices, critical and biographical articles, and books on kindred subjects, I have had to reject hundreds of items, usually by relying on a subjective judgment of significance to my hypothetical "serious reader." One obvious result is that recent criticism is more fully represented here than is earlier commentary, although no single year's work has been listed in its entirety. Again, I have not attempted to include every item which may be found in the very useful bibliographies and bibliographical essays cited in this volume.

More specifically, I have excluded from consideration all M.A. theses and Ph.D. dissertations except those that appeared (and that are cited) as articles and books. Original theses and dissertations are discussed at length elsewhere, in bibliographical essays, chapters, and listings described in this *Reference Guide*. (*See* especially 1969.B13; 1975.B2; 1975.B6.) Omitted also are standard reference works such as encyclopedias, handbooks, introductions to the study of English and American literature, and bibliographical listings in specialized periodicals such as *American Literature*. In the treatment of anthologies and editions of Adams's works, on the other hand, I have attempted to include some discussion of introductions, headnotes, and editorial notes whenever these editorial additions to the texts could lay claim to independent critical value. Final judgment in every instance was my own; and I am aware that the results will not satisfy every reader. Although my aim throughout has been usefulness and not completeness, I of course remain responsible for any deficiency.

I wish to thank Kay Orrill and Lynda Boren for their help in completing this volume and the Tulane University Council on Research for financial support.

Major Writings by Henry Adams

CHAPTERS OF ERIE AND OTHER ESSAYS (with Charles F. Adams, Jr.). Boston: James R. Osgood and Co., 1871.

ESSAYS IN ANGLO-SAXON LAW (edited by Henry Adams). Boston: Little, Brown and Co., 1876.

DOCUMENTS RELATING TO NEW ENGLAND FEDERALISM (edited by Henry Adams). Boston: Little, Brown and Co., 1877.

THE LIFE OF ALBERT GALLATIN. Philadelphia: J. B. Lippincott and Co., 1879.

DEMOCRACY: AN AMERICAN NOVEL (Anon.). New York: Henry Holt and Co., 1880.

JOHN RANDOLPH. Boston: Houghton Mifflin Co., 1882.

ESTHER: A NOVEL. (Pseudonym, Frances Snow Compton.) New York: Henry Holt and Co., 1884.

HISTORY OF THE UNITED STATES DURING THE ADMINISTRATIONS OF THOMAS JEFFERSON AND JAMES MADISON. 9 Vols. New York: Charles Scribner's Sons, 1889-1891.

HISTORICAL ESSAYS. New York: Charles Scribner's Sons, 1891.

MEMOIRS OF MARAU TAAROA LAST QUEEN OF TAHITI. Privately printed, Washington, D. C., 1893.

MEMOIRS OF ARII TAIMAI E MARAMA OF EIMEO TERIIRERE OF TOORAAI TERIINUI OF TAHITI. (Pseudonym, Tauraatua I Amo.) Privately printed, Paris, 1901.

A LETTER TO AMERICAN TEACHERS OF HISTORY. Privately printed, Baltimore: J. H. Furst and Co., 1910.

THE LIFE OF GEORGE CABOT LODGE. Boston: Houghton Mifflin Co., 1911.

Major Writings by Henry Adams

MONT-SAINT-MICHEL AND CHARTRES. Boston: Houghton Mifflin Co., 1913.

THE EDUCATION OF HENRY ADAMS. Boston: Houghton Mifflin Co., 1918.

For a complete list of the writings of Henry Adams, *see* the three volumes of Ernest Samuels' biography (1948.A1; 1958.A1; 1964.A1).

Writings about Henry Adams, 1879-1975

1879 A BOOKS - NONE

1879 B SHORTER WRITINGS

1 ANON. Review of The Life of Albert Gallatin. Nation, 29 (21 August), 128-29.
Book is not for general reader, ponderous and intimidating in size alone. Reviewer feels that biography is most successful when Adams "cuts loose" from Gallatin and speaks in his own voice. For attribution to Charles Francis Adams, Jr., see 1950.B6.

2 ANON. Review of The Life of Albert Gallatin. Nation, 29 (28 August), 144-45.
Bulk of material is tedious, incredibly dull. Finds some redeeming merit in Adams's spirited interpretation of historical materials. For attribution to Charles Francis Adams, Jr., see 1950.B6.

1880 A BOOKS - NONE

1880 B SHORTER WRITINGS

1 ANON. Review of Democracy. Appleton's Journal (June), p. 575.
Sophisticated review. Finds the novel "extremely amusing" but doubts that its "reformatory value is any greater than that of other methods which are mercilessly ridiculed in it."

2 ANON. Review of Democracy. Atlantic Monthly, 46 (September), 421-22.
Finds the novel rather narrow and inconclusive largely due to the limitations of the heroine. Mrs. Lightfoot Lee is "scarcely qualified to discover the secret of democracy."

1880

3 ANON. Review of *Democracy*. Chicago *Dial*, 1 (May), 11-12.
Concentrates on style of author. Praises wit and graceful form of novel. "Story proceeds in a natural and consistent method."

4 ANON. Review of *Democracy*. *Harper's New Monthly Magazine*, 61 (July), 314.
"A clever but exaggerated satire on social and political life in Washington, rather than a novel."

5 ANON. Review of *Democracy*. *Nation*, 30 (22 April), 312.
Unfavorable review. "Cardinal defect" is that "the love story and the political satire are not better blended." For attribution to William Cary Brownell, *see* 1958.A1.

6 ANON. Review of *Democracy*. *The New York Times* (11 April), p. 10.
Mainly laudatory in manner. Praises author for his "cleverness" and "vigorous" expression.

7 ANON. Review of *Democracy*. *Scribner's Monthly* (July), pp. 474-75.
Critical of style and form of novel, while finding it a worthwhile social document.

1882 A BOOKS - NONE

1882 B SHORTER WRITINGS

1 ANON. Review of *Democracy*. *Academy*, no. 503 (July), p. 5.
Welcomes "this English edition of *Democracy*." The book is "so clever" that it might be the work of Henry James or Anthony Trollope.

2 ANON. Review of *Democracy*. *Athenaeum* (24 June), p. 795.
Claims that the writer "derived the idea of his story from 'Le Nabab' and 'Son Excellence Eugene Rougon.'" "There is no doubt of the writer's earnestness or of the skill with which he has contrived that his *tendenz* should not interfere with the artistic excellence of *his tale*."

3 ANON. Review of *Democracy*. *Blackwood's Edinburgh Magazine*, 31 (May), 577-92.
The characters are "not very original" but the "book is extremely honest in its objective."

4 ANON. Review of *Democracy*. *Edinburgh Review*, 156 (July), 189-203.

Treats the book as a scathing satire, not to be taken as representative of the majority of American people.

5 ANON. "A Political Satire." New York Semi-Weekly Tribune (1 August), n.p.
A review of Democracy. Discusses book's reception in England. Credits fine style of the work for its popularity. Largely satirical review; praises Democracy while undercutting British snobbery. "It is distinguished by an ease and smartness in which English fiction is apt to be especially deficient."

6 ANON. Review of John Randolph. New York Semi-Weekly Tribune (20 October), p. 4.
Criticizes tone of book as being "provokingly superior" but sees it as a "lively and interesting volume."

7 ANON. Review of Democracy. Saturday Review, 54 (8 July), 55-56.
Laudatory review; praises work as containing "wit, good sense."

8 ANON. Review of Democracy. Westminster Review, 118 (October), 281.
Mixed opinion, finding "Promise greater than its performance." "Chief merit is its demonstration of an intimate knowledge of the machinery of American politics."

9 WARD, MARY A. British review of Democracy. Fortnightly Review, 38 (1 July), 78-93.
Concerned with reception of the novel in England. Finds fault with "want of finish," and praises "dexterity" and "imaginative power." Cites "Mr. Henry Brooks Adams" as probable author based on comparison with "Civil Service Reform" (1869).

1884 A BOOKS - NONE

1884 B SHORTER WRITINGS

1 ANON. Review of Democracy. Saturday Review (2 February), pp. 154-55.
Sees the novel as merely clever. Compares it to John Hay's The Bread-Winners (1884) which, according to the reviewer, shows more depth in its criticisms of American life.

1885

1885 A BOOKS - NONE

1885 B SHORTER WRITINGS

1 ANON. Review of _Esther_. _Athenaeum_ (25 July), pp. 107-108.
Reviewer finds the book "wanting in human interest."

1886 A BOOKS - NONE

1886 B SHORTER WRITINGS

1 DEVILLE, EDWARD. "Oliver Wendell Holmes." _Fortnightly Review_, 46 (August), 235-43.
Reviews Holmes's writing, stressing "amiable" qualities of satire in contrast with _Democracy_ (without mentioning Adams).

1889 A BOOKS - NONE

1889 B SHORTER WRITINGS

1 ANON. Review of _The History of the United States During the First Administration of Thomas Jefferson_. _Nation_, 49 (12 December), 480-83.
Lucid treatment of development of Jeffersonian democracy. Praises work for its thoroughness and skill in the depiction of famous historical personalities.

2 ANON. Review of _The History of the United States During the First Administration of Thomas Jefferson_. _Nation_, 49 (19 December), 504-506.
Reviewer feels that Adams could have devoted more attention to the debate between the Federalists and Jefferson at the time of the occupation at New Orleans.

3 ANON. Review of _The History of the United States During the First Administration of Thomas Jefferson_. _The New York Times_ (27 October), p. 19.
Although cold in its treatment, the work shows an admirable style. Reviewer labels it a historical work "of great importance."

1890

1890 A BOOKS - NONE

1890 B SHORTER WRITINGS

1 ANON. Review of The History of the United States During the Administrations of Thomas Jefferson. Critic, 13 (5 April), 164.
A generally favorable review. Finds Adams a competent, impartial historian.

2 ANON. Review of The History of the United States During the Administrations of Thomas Jefferson. English Historical Review, 8:802-806.
Mr. Adams is "...too earnest and convinced a patriot to maintain an attitude of severe impartiality to all questions."

3 ANON. Review of The History of the United States During the First Administration of Thomas Jefferson. Harper's New Monthly Magazine, 80 (May), 968-69.
Praises Adams's work for its perfect perspective. Treatment of Jefferson is seen to be fair. Adams gives a humorous touch and "aesthetic beauty" to the historical intrigues of Burr's conspiracy.

4 ANON. Review of The History of the United States During the Second Administration of Thomas Jefferson. Nation, 50 (8 May), 376-78.
Extensive quotes. Laudatory review. Praises Adams for his impartial accuracy.

5 ANON. Review of The History of the United States During the Second Administration of Thomas Jefferson. Nation, 50 (15 May), 395-97.
Extensive quotes. Feels that Adams's summary of results of embargo acts is "calm and philosophical."

6 ANON. Review of The History of the United States During the Second Administration of Thomas Jefferson. The New York Times (9 February), p. 19.
Sees book as extremely well-written, while there is a "want of sympathy in his account of Jefferson."

7 ANON. Review of The History of the United States During the First Administration of James Madison. London Critic, 14 (8 November), 229.
First volume is praised for its "undaunted scholarship," the second for its humor. "Little as the author meant it,

as a comic story, his second volume has afforded us more fun than a critic usually gets out of solemn history."

8 ANON. Review of The History of the United States During the First Administration of James Madison. Nation, 51 (20 November), 405-407.
Blames dullness of earlier portion of work on the figure of Madison himself.

9 ANON. Review of The History of the United States During the First Administration of James Madison. Nation, 51 (27 November), 424-26.
Too much emphasis placed upon John Randolph as the "Tragic Chorus" in order to accentuate the moral lesson of the story.

10 [THURSTON, H. W.] Review of The History of the United States During the Administrations of Thomas Jefferson. Chicago Dial, 11 (June), 33-35.
"Mr. Adams has done his work well, so well that there will be no need for another to do it again."

1891 A BOOKS - NONE

1891 B SHORTER WRITINGS

1 ANON. Review of The History of the United States During the Second Administration of James Madison. London Critic, 15 (28 February), 106.
"No works in American historical literature . . . combine so many merits and display such power."

2 ANON. Review of The History of the United States During the Second Administration of James Madison. Nation, 52 (16 April), 322-23.
Work lacks interest because it is tedious reading.

3 ANON. Review of The History of the United States During the Second Administration of James Madison. Nation, 52 (23 April), 344-45.
"Although we may disagree with Adams's interpretation, his accuracy in presenting the facts is unquestionable."

4 ANON. Review of The History of the United States During the Administrations of James Madison. The New York Times (1 March), p. 19.
Calls the work "fresh" and "stimulating" if sometimes "pessimistic."

1897 A BOOKS - NONE

1897 B SHORTER WRITINGS

1 LA FARGE, JOHN. An Artist's Letters from Japan. New York: The Century Co., passim.
Henry Adams identified as "A," the travel companion of La Farge, who comments on what they experience.

1898 A BOOKS - NONE

1898 B SHORTER WRITINGS

1 ANON. "Henry Adams," in Report of the Class of 1858 of Harvard College. Boston: Alfred Mudge and Son, pp. 6-7.
Brief biography.

1913 A BOOKS - NONE

1913 B SHORTER WRITINGS

1 ANON. Review of Mont-Saint-Michel and Chartres. Booklist, 10 (February), 215.
Laudatory review. "A careful and loving study." "A work by a scholar, primarily for scholars."

2 CRAM, RALPH ADAMS. "Editor's Note," [sometimes reprinted as "Introduction"] in Mont-Saint-Michel and Chartres. Edited by Ralph Adams Cram. Boston and New York: Houghton Mifflin Co., pp. v-viii.
Describes circumstances of general publication of Chartres by the American Institute of Architects, including their "action . . . in making Mr. Adams an Honorary Member."

3 HESSELGRAVE, CHARLES E. "A Holiday Trip into the Land of Books." Independent (11 December), p. 510.
Calls Mont-Saint-Michel and Chartres a "brilliant and penetrating study." Praises "sumptuous" beauty of book.

4 LODGE, HENRY CABOT. Early Memories. New York: Charles Scribner's Sons, passim.
Lodge's commentary on his long relationship with Henry Adams, which began when Adams was his history teacher at Harvard.

1914

1914 A BOOKS - NONE

1914 B SHORTER WRITINGS

1 ANON. "The Romance of the Middle Ages." *Nation*, 98 (5 March), 239-40.
Review of *Mont-Saint-Michel and Chartres*. Despite some slight inaccuracies the book is beautifully written, quite erudite and sensitive.

2 LUQUIENS, FREDERICK BLISS. Review of *Mont-Saint-Michel and Chartres*. *Yale Review*, 3 (June), 826-30.
Review seeks to put book in its proper perspective as an imaginative, mystical approach to medieval expression.

3 TAYLOR, HENRY OSBORN. Review of *Mont-Saint-Michel and Chartres*. *American Historical Review*, 19 (April), 592-94.
Sensitive review that seeks to distinguish the reality of the Middle Ages from Adams's reaction to its architecture and religion. We "are left in doubt whether we have gone the round of the twelfth and thirteenth centuries, or the round of the mind of Henry Adams."

1915 A BOOKS - NONE

1915 B SHORTER WRITINGS

1 THAYER, WILLIAM ROSCOE. *Life and Letters of John Hay*. 2 Vols. Boston and New York: Houghton Mifflin Co., passim.
Sheds light on Henry Adams's close friendship with Hay; Vol. II contains letters to Adams.

1918 A BOOKS - NONE

1918 B SHORTER WRITINGS

1 ANON. "At Mr. Adams'." *The New Republic* (25 May), pp. 106-108.
"The 'instinct for workmanship' was strong in him, and his work was most of all to understand." Concentrates on the *Education* to show that "his standard was impossibly high."

2 [MORE, PAUL ELMER]. Review of the *Education*. *The Unpartizan Review*, 10 (October-December), 255-72.

Finds "moral of the book": "the baffled sense of mystery behind the veil of apparent design." Biographical emphasis; Henry Adams "was *par excellence* the pure Romantic, yet withal a New Englander at heart, not a German." Some consideration of *Chartres*.

3 TAYLOR, HENRY OSBORN. "The Education of Henry Adams." *Atlantic Monthly*, 122:484-91.

Review of the *Education*, with some consideration of other works. "Perhaps no other American has left such a mass of clever writing . . . and has died so unrecognized by the public, educated or otherwise." Quotes extensively from the *Education*, noting events and people described there: " . . . they come to him in retrospection." Includes anecdotes of Adams and his friends, and points out that the *Education* omits much, as the author is "conscientiously posing as the spirit of a New England Montaigne."

1919 A BOOKS - NONE

1919 B SHORTER WRITINGS

1 ADAMS, BROOKS. "The Heritage of Henry Adams," in *The Degradation of the Democratic Dogma*. New York: Macmillan Co., pp. 1-122.

Discusses Henry Adams's ideas with attention to his intellectual kinship with John Quincy Adams, with whom he shared a special set of interests and abilities. Reprinted: 1969.B4.

2 ELIOT, T. S. "A Sceptical Patrician." *Athenaeum* (23 May), pp. 361-362.

Reviews the *Education* and warns: "It is doubtful whether the book ought to be called an autobiography, for there is far too little of the author in it." Reprinted: 1962.B5.

1920 A BOOKS - NONE

1920 B SHORTER WRITINGS

1 BECKER, CARL. Review of *The Degradation of the Democratic Dogma*. *The American Historical Review*, 25 (April), 480-82.

"The three essays of Henry Adams . . . form a valuable supplement to the *Education*," as parts of his "intelligible philosophy of history." Raises questions about Adams's

1920

naive acceptance of the dogmas of natural science: and about his "scientific(?) . . . attitude" toward history.

2 COOK, ALBERT STANBURROUGH. "Six Letters of Henry Adams." Yale Review, 10 (October), 131-40.
Previously unpublished letters concerning Chartres. Brief editorial comments.

3 FORD, WORTHINGTON CHAUNCEY. "Introductory Note" to A Cycle of Adams Letters. Edited by Worthington Chauncey Ford. 2 Vols. Boston and New York: Houghton Mifflin Co., pp. vii-xiv.
Calls attention to Henry Adams's "self-drawn representation of himself as a 'failure' in the Education, which "awakens astonishment and challenges examination." Reprinted: 1968.B5.

4 LA FARGE, MABEL HOOPER. "Henry Adams: A Niece's Memories," in Letters to a Niece and Prayer to the Virgin of Chartres. Boston: Houghton Mifflin Co., pp. 3-27.
Personal view of Henry Adams as a shy, reserved avuncular figure, very different from the hero of The Education of Henry Adams.

5 LUQUIENS, FREDERICK BLISS. "Seventeen Letters of Henry Adams." Yale Review, 10 (October), 111-30.
Previously unpublished, these letters and the short introduction discuss Chartres and medieval history and illustrate the depth of Adams's scholarship.

6 S., J. W. N. [J. W. N. SULLIVAN]. Review of The Degradation of the Democratic Dogma. Athenaeum (21 May), p. 665.
Review concentrates on his imprecise use of technical vocabulary: "Failure to distinguish between the different meanings a word may have is more marked . . . with some people than with others, but it can seldom have been more complete than it was with Henry Adams." "A criticism of his writings is really a criticism of his employment of certain key-words. From such an examination we can construct his mental processes."

7 SHERMAN, STUART P. "Evolution in the Adams Family." Nation, 110 (10 April), 473-77.
Studies Henry Adams as fourth-generation member of Adams family with special attention to the principle of "degradation of energy" and heavy reliance on the Education.

1921 A BOOKS - NONE

1921 B SHORTER WRITINGS

1 LAUGHLIN, J. LAURENCE. "Some Recollections of Henry Adams." *Scribner's Magazine*, 69 (May), 576-85.
Based on memories of Henry Adams's former student at Harvard.

2 MORE, PAUL ELMER. "Henry Adams," in *A New England Group and Others*. Boston and New York: Houghton Mifflin Co., pp. 115-40.
Considers the *Education* as an exercise in "sentimental nihilism," lacking in the "manlier" qualities which also characterized New England in his time.

1922 A BOOKS - NONE

1922 B SHORTER WRITINGS

1 BRUCE, WILLIAM CABELL. *John Randolph of Roanoke, 1773-1833*. 2 Vols. New York: G. P. Putnam's Sons, passim.
"Preface" and text attempt to correct Henry Adams's portrait in *John Randolph*, which Bruce finds "is really nothing but a family pamphlet, saturated with sectional prejudices and antipathies of the year 1882."

2 FORD, WORTHINGTON CHAUNCEY. "The Adams Family." *Quarterly Review*, 237 (April), 298-312.
Reviews six books, including the *Education*, *Chartres*, *Chapters of Erie*, and others by family members. All provide evidence of the family "habit of self-examination."

3 SHAFER, ROBERT. *Progress and Science*. New Haven: Yale University Press, pp. 155-93.
Chapter IV, "Science and History," considers the relationship of Henry Adams's ideas about science to those of his grandfather John Quincy Adams. Concentrates on the *Education* and "Letter to American Teachers of History," to reveal "the suicidal conclusions of Henry Adams, of any sober evaluation of the relations of modern science to human life." Henry Adams's "vision was consistently outward into the world of practical activity. . . . But complete outwardness of vision is a fatal bar to the understanding of men."

1923

1923 A BOOKS - NONE

1923 B SHORTER WRITINGS

1 HOLT, HENRY. Garrulities of An Octogenarian Editor. Boston and New York: Houghton Mifflin, passim.
Discusses the circumstances surrounding Henry Adams's secret authorship of Democracy and Esther.

1924 A BOOKS - NONE

1924 B SHORTER WRITINGS

1 SABINE, GEORGE H. "Henry Adams and the Writing of History." University of California Chronicle, 26 (January), 31-46.
Concentrates on the Education, with frequent references to Chartres and other examples of historical writing, to prove that Adams "stands for something that is truly typical of our time, for a puzzlement that affects us all, each in his own way and degree." To Adams, "complexity and lack of order" in historical fact and in modern life "became a torture" which he endured with a philosophy of "moral skepticism." His "sense of repression and oppression . . . forms the constant theme of Adams' autobiography."

2 SPEARE, MORRIS EDMUND. The Political Novel: Its Development in England and America. New York: Oxford University Press, passim.
Summarizes the story of Democracy and discusses its author's "political philosophy" (p. 299). Henry Adams's views parallel those of Woodrow Wilson. Chapter XII: "The Pioneer American Political Novel of Henry Adams."

1926 A BOOKS - NONE

1926 B SHORTER WRITINGS

1 BEACH, JOSEPH WARREN. The Outlook For American Prose. Chicago: University of Chicago Press, pp. 202-14.
Concentrates on the Education to establish the debt of Sherwood Anderson to Henry Adams.

2 MUMFORD, LEWIS. The Golden Day. New York: Boni and Liveright, pp. 217-25.
Considers Henry Adams as: "a historian" who spoke for his generation and "a victim of the theological [Puritan]

notion of eternity--the notion that our present life is significant or rational only if it can be prolonged." "The truth is, Henry Adams's generation had forfeited its desires, and it was at loose ends."

1927 A BOOKS - NONE

1927 B SHORTER WRITINGS

1 COMMAGER, HENRY STEELE. "Henry Adams." South Atlantic Quarterly, 26 (July), 252-65.
" . . . the tragedy of Henry Adams was that he was born out of his time." Partly biographical, relying on the Education. Surveys other writings: " . . . within its scope the History is definitive," and concentrates on Adams's "fascinating" mind. Chartres "is the most perfect thing Henry Adams ever wrote."

2 PARRINGTON, VERNON LOUIS. The Beginnings of Critical Realism in America. Vol. III of Main Currents in American Thought. New York: Harcourt Brace, esp. pp. 214-27.
Seeks to account for the habitual "skepticism of the house of Adams," particularly as it shows itself in the Education and in Henry Adams's life. Emphasizes Henry Adams's "failure to take into account the economic springs of action" in his work.

1928 A BOOKS - NONE

1928 B SHORTER WRITINGS

1 ELLIOTT, W. Y. The Pragmatic Revolt in Politics. New York: Macmillan, p. 39.
Footnote 19 discusses the intellectual differences between Henry Adams and Henry James.

2 WHIPPLE, T. K. Spokesmen. New York: D. Appleton and Co., pp. 23-44.
Selects Henry Adams as one of ten Americans who poetically expressed their dissatisfaction with "practical society" and the failure of American life. Reprinted: 1965.B18.

Writings about Henry Adams, 1879-1975

1929

1929 A BOOKS - NONE

1929 B SHORTER WRITINGS

1 ADAMS, JAMES TRUSLOW. "Henry Adams and the New Physics." *Yale Review*, 19 (December), 283-302.
Quarrels with assessment of Henry Adams as "a brilliant amateur" by recounting his attempts "to formulate a theory of history. . . ." Special attention to essays, *History*, *Chartres*, and *Education*, studied in light of modern physics.

1930 A BOOKS - NONE

1930 B SHORTER WRITINGS

1 ADAMS, JAMES TRUSLOW. *The Adams Family*. Boston: Little, Brown, and Co., pp. 305-51.
Henry Adams included in "The Fourth Generation." Mainly biographical.

2 BEARD, CHARLES A. and MARY. *The Rise of American Civilization*. Combined edition. 2 Vols. New York: Macmillan, passim.
Echoes of the *Education* appear in both volumes.

3 FORD, WORTHINGTON CHAUNCEY, ed. *Letters of Henry Adams (1858-1891)*. Vol. 1. Boston: Houghton Mifflin. First of two vols.
Editor's "Note" calls attention to the limitations of *The Education of Henry Adams* as only a partial portrait of Henry Adams, which this collection of letters is intended to supplement. (*See* 1938.B2.)

1931 A BOOKS - NONE

1931 B SHORTER WRITINGS

1 BLACKMUR, R. P. "The Failure of Henry Adams." *Hound and Horn*, 4 (April-June), 440-46.
Reviews Henry Adams's *Letters* (1930) in terms of the meaning of "failure to the artist and the man."

2 MacDONALD, WILLIAM. "Adams," in *American Writers on American Literature*. Edited by John Macy. New York: Horace Liveright, Inc., pp. 317-26.
Summarizes Henry Adams's career as that of an "eccentric," divided between work as "a historian and biographer,"

and the thought of "an intellectual something for which a single comprehensive label is not easily found." History, Chartres, and the Education receive special attention.

1932 A BOOKS - NONE

1932 B SHORTER WRITINGS

1 LEWISOHN, LUDWIG. Expression in America. New York: Harper & Brothers, passim.

Finds Democracy a failure as literature (but not as political criticism); while the Education is "not only a great but a crucial book, a classic of both American literature and American life" (p. 347).

1933 A BOOKS

1 ADAMS, JAMES TRUSLOW. Henry Adams. New York: Boni, Inc.

Pioneer biography which closely follows the outlines of the Education. Includes a "Bibliography of the Writings of Henry Adams," later superseded by Samuels. See 1948.A1; 1958.A1; 1964.A1.

1933 B SHORTER WRITINGS

1 HICKS, GRANVILLE. The Great Tradition. New York: Macmillan Co., passim.

Concentrates on Democracy and the Education, claiming that Henry Adams never learned enough to keep him from "naively adopting the attitudes of his class" (p. 72). The Education Adams wrote "merely to amuse himself" (p. 139). Reprinted: 1969.B3.

1934 A BOOKS - NONE

1934 B SHORTER WRITINGS

1 BIXLER, PAUL H. "A Note on Henry Adams." Colophon, part 17, Item #2, n.p.

A brief discussion of some late Adams letters and marginal notations in some of the books which Adams donated to the library at Western Reserve University. One letter, dated February 17, 1918, expresses a definite sense of Adams's hopelessness before chaos, which seems to have been with him at the end.

2 CHANLER, MRS. WINTHROP. Roman Spring: Memoirs. Boston: Little, Brown, and Co., pp. 212-13, 291-308.
Recalls the "Friendship of Henry Adams" (Chapter 25) and discusses his interest in Catholicism, especially in relation to Chartres. Concentrates on Henry Adams's last years and on his attitudes toward Mrs. Adams's death.

3 SHUMATE, ROBERT V. "The Political Philosophy of Henry Adams." American Political Science Review, 28 (August), 599-610.
As a "second Aristotle," Henry Adams should be studied to determine his "philosophy of history" and its "political implications." "It would be difficult to show that Henry Adams ever had a complete and coherent theory of government"; "his approach to political questions was generally ethical rather than narrowly partisan," and his use of science was "one-sided."

4 WECTER, DIXON. "The Harvard Exiles." Virginia Quarterly Review, 10 (April), 244-57.
Although focused on T. S. Eliot, the essay describes similarities in thought among Eliot, Santayana, and Henry Adams--all "examples of that remarkable type, the pure academic tory."

1935 A BOOKS - NONE

1935 B SHORTER WRITINGS

1 NICHOLS, ROY F. "The Dynamic Interpretation of History." New England Quarterly, 8 (June), 163-78.
Examines the validity of Henry Adams's "dynamic theory" with reference to the discoveries during the "veritable revolution" in science since the Education and late essays were written. Finds that Adams's challenge to teachers of history to seek a dynamic interpretation still stands, even though his own attempt to formulate it must now be discarded.

1936 A BOOKS - NONE

1936 B SHORTER WRITINGS

1 BLACKMUR, R. P. "The Expense of Greatness: Three Emphases on Henry Adams." Virginia Quarterly Review, 12 (July), 396-415.
Biographical observations based on as yet unpublished materials. Reprinted: 1940.B2; 1955.B3.

2 SIMONDS, KATE. "The Tragedy of Mrs. Henry Adams." New England Quarterly, 9 (December), 564-82.
Examines the life of Marian Hooper Adams with special attention to Henry Adams's letters, Esther, Democracy, the Education, and other sources. Effects of her marriage to Henry Adams receive consideration, as does the impact of her suicide on him. Views Chartres as a monument to the memory of Mrs. Adams.

3 THORON, WARD. "Preface" to The Letters of Mrs. Henry Adams, 1865-1883. Edited by Ward Thoron. Boston: Little, Brown, and Co., pp. vii-xv.
Discusses relationship of Henry Adams and his wife. "Appendix VI," pp. 483-488, gathers together materials concerned with Democracy.

1937 A BOOKS - NONE

1937 B SHORTER WRITINGS

1 BAYM, MAX I. "William James and Henry Adams." New England Quarterly, 10 (December), 717-42.
Examination of Henry Adams's marginalia to show something of the influence of William James on Adams's thought.

2 BLUNT, HUGH F. "Mal-Education of Henry Adams." Catholic World, 145 (April), 46-52.
Uses passages from Chartres to document the assertion that "its whole theme leaves us gasping at its blasphemy." " . . . certainly he [Adams] was not equipped to write about the Catholic Church."

3 COMMAGER, HENRY STEELE. "Henry Adams," in The Marcus W. Jernegan Essays in American Historiography. Edited by William T. Hutchinson. Chicago: University of Chicago Press, pp. 191-206.
Treats Henry Adams's life and career as a historian: "Adams made it a rule to ask questions he couldn't answer--questions which were, perhaps, unanswerable . . . Adams illuminates, better than any of his contemporaries, the course of American history."

4 KRAUS, MICHAEL. A History of American History. New York: Farrar and Rinehart, pp. 321-35, and passim.
Assesses Henry Adams's career as a historian, with special emphasis on History, which is analyzed volume by volume, and heavy reliance on Henry Adams's letters of the

period. Kraus's judgment: "one of the highest achievements in American historiography." Traces Henry Adams's influence on other historians.

1938 A BOOKS - NONE

1938 B SHORTER WRITINGS

1 BAYM, MAX I. "The 1858 Catalogue of Henry Adams's Library." Colophon, n.s. 3 (Autumn), 483-89.
Lists books in Henry Adams's undergraduate library.

2 FORD, WORTHINGTON CHAUNCEY, ed. Letters of Henry Adams (1892-1918). Boston: Houghton Mifflin.
Second of two vols. (See 1930.B3.)

3 HICKS, GRANVILLE. "The Letters of Henry Adams." The New Masses (25 October), pp. 357-62.
Adams's letters of his last 26 years sustain "the precise mood of the Education." He knew that "only the Marxists looked at events as he did."

4 TATE, ALLEN. "The Crisis," Part Two, in The Fathers. New York: G. P. Putnam's Sons, p. 121.
Fictional treatment of Henry Adams: " . . . among these a young man to be better known later, Henry Adams, a great snob even then, who got on Charles's nerves by pretending friendship with Rooney Lee, the Colonel's son, having been with him at Harvard, and yet ridiculing him for his lack of learning." Echoes the Education. Reprinted: 1970.B7.

5 WINTERS, YVOR. Maule's Curse. Norfolk, Conn.: New Directions, pp. 173-74.
Touches upon Henry Adams's life in order to show that, "In Henry Adams we see the curse at work most clearly . . . he propounded the aesthetic theory that modern art must be confused to express confusion. . . ." Reprinted: 1943.B5; 1947.B9.

1939 A BOOKS - NONE

1939 B SHORTER WRITINGS

1 KRONENBERGER, LOUIS. "The Education of Henry Adams: The Sixth of the Books That Changed Our Minds." The New Republic, 98 (15 March), 155-58.

"Although the present moment is not congenial . . . to the Education . . . it may be that Adams has taught us more in autobiography than he could have in action."

2 _____. "The Education of Henry Adams: The Sixth of the Books That Changed Our Minds," in Books That Changed Our Minds. Edited by Malcolm Cowley and Bernard Smith. New York: Kelmscott Editions, pp. 45-57.
Reprints 1939.B1.

1940 A BOOKS - NONE

1940 B SHORTER WRITINGS

1 BLACKMUR, R. P. "Henry Adams: Three Late Moments." Kenyon Review, 2 (Winter), 7-29.
Biographical sidelights on Henry Adams's last years. Reprinted: 1967.B4.

2 _____. The Expense of Greatness. New York: Arrow, pp. 253-76.
Reprint of 1936.B1.

3 CARGILL, OSCAR. "The Mediaevalism of Henry Adams," in Essays and Studies in Honor of Carleton Brown. New York: New York University Press, pp. 296-329.
Draws heavily on Henry Adams's letters and the Education to discuss Adams's view; makes special use of historical reviews of editor Adams in the North American Review and of Essays in Anglo-Saxon Law.

4 HOLT, W. STULL. "The Idea of Scientific History in America." Journal of the History of Ideas, 1 (January), 352-62.
Surveys assumptions and developments of scientific history in America, with attention to Henry Adams's standing among his contemporaries. In 1940, "scientific history" still seems possible; "no generally accepted verdict can as yet be said to have been rendered."

5 SCHRIFTGIESSER, KARL. "The Admirable Adams," in Families. New York: Howell, Soskin, pp. 11-54.
Henry Adams studied in context of family history and family thought: "The Admirable Adams." Shows influence of economic interests of the 1930's and colored by the account of Henry Adams's life in The Education of Henry Adams.

1941

1941 A BOOKS - NONE

1941 B SHORTER WRITINGS

1 CARGILL, OSCAR. Intellectual America: Ideas on the March. New York: Macmillan, esp. pp. 551-69.
As a part of his intellectual assessment of "The Freudians," Cargill briefly reviews Henry Adams's life and writings, with special attention to the novels, Chartres, and the Education, stressing the influence of Joris-Karl Huysmans and "mariolatry." " . . . honest self-recrimination" is "the epitome of Henry Adams" (p. 569).

2 ELSEY, GEORGE McKEE. "The First Education of Henry Adams." New England Quarterly, 14 (December), 679-84.
Largely biographical; includes the short autobiography which Henry Adams drafted for inclusion in his Harvard "Class Book of 1858" and shows that it is very different from the Education.

3 HUME, ROBERT A. "Henry Adams's Quest for Certainty," in Stanford Studies in Language and Literature. Edited by Hardin Craig. Stanford: Stanford University Press, pp. 361-73.
Close study of the last chapters of the Education and the "dynamic theory of history"(in Chartres and "A Letter to the American Teachers of History")leads to "serious demurrers" concerning its validity. Overall, the claim of the Education to "classic" status remains "questionable."

4 JORDY, WILLIAM H. "Henry Adams and Walt Whitman." South Atlantic Quarterly, 60 (April), 132-45.
Henry Adams could have met Whitman only during 1868-69, "when both were in Washington." Adams's "two mentions" of Whitman represent "high compliments."

5 MITCHELL, STEWART. "Henry Adams and Some of His Students." Proceedings, Massachusetts Historical Society, 66 (1936-1941), 294-312.
Reviews Henry Adams's six-year career as teacher of History at Harvard, correcting impressions created by the Education. Includes class records and comments from Adams's former students, who are described in brief biographies.

1942 A BOOKS - NONE

1942 B SHORTER WRITINGS

1 EDWARDS, HERBERT. "The Prophetic Mind of Henry Adams." College English, 3 (May), 708-21.
Uses letters and the Education to show that Adams "predicted the first and second world wars" and "was a full generation ahead of his time in his disillusionment with the ideals of the Industrial Revolution. . . ." Traces literary judgment and the influence of Adams's thought. "He was a poet in Matthew Arnold's sense--an artist, a philosopher, and a prophet whose work was a criticism of life."

2 GLICKSBERG, CHARLES I. "Henry Adams Reports on a Trades-Union Meeting." New England Quarterly, 15 (December), 724-28.
Previously unpublished report to the U. S. State Department edited and printed.

3 NUHN, FERNER. The Wind Blew from the East: A Study in the Orientation of American Culture. New York: Harper & Brothers, pp. 164-94.
Concentrates on polarities in thought and writing of Henry Adams, who remains "not quite the artist."

1943 A BOOKS - NONE

1943 B SHORTER WRITINGS

1 BEARD, CHARLES A. "Historians at Work: Brooks and Henry Adams." Atlantic Monthly, 171 (April), 87-93.
Reviews the cooperative efforts of Brooks and Henry Adams in shaping The Law of Civilization and Decay, "one of the outstanding documents of intellectual history in the United States and, in a way, the Western world"--"the first extended attempt on the part of an American thinker to reduce universal history, or at least Western history, to a single formula or body of formulas conceived in the spirit of modern science." Based on "Adams manuscripts," especially Henry Adams's "annotations" in Brooks's personal copies of the Law.

2 _____. "Introduction" to The Law of Civilization and Decay: An Essay on History by Brooks Adams. New York: Knopf.
An account of the collaboration between Brooks and Henry Adams, based on their correspondence, 1893-1906, while the

Law was being planned, written, and revised, and later translated into French. Supplements Brooks Adams's "Introduction" to The Degradation of the Democratic Dogma and discusses Henry Adams's essay "The Tendency of History" in detail.

3 BLACKMUR, R. P. "The Novels of Henry Adams." Sewanee Review, 51 (April), 281-304.

Claims that Henry Adams's novels, "unlike those of a professional novelist, do not show their full significance except in connection with his life." The two novels do have common themes, such as feminine superiority, which show up "twenty years later" in the Education. Reprinted: 1967.B4.

4 WILSON, EDMUND. "Introduction" to reprinting of Henry Adams's Life of George Cabot Lodge, in The Shock of Recognition. Edited by Edmund Wilson. Garden City: Doubleday, Doran and Co., Inc., pp. 742-46.

Finds Lodge "the most uncanny example of Adams's equivocal attitude in relation to the social world of Boston and to the official world of Washington. . . ."

5 WINTERS, YVOR. "Henry Adams or The Creation of Confusion," in The Anatomy of Nonsense. Norfolk: New Directions.

Declares the Chartres and the Education evidence of Henry Adams's "radical disintegration of mind." Reprints 1938.B5. Reprinted: 1947.B9.

1944 A BOOKS - NONE

1944 B SHORTER WRITINGS

1 BAYM, MAX I. "Henry Adams and Henry Vignaud." New England Quarterly, 17 (September), 442-49.

Three unpublished letters to Vignaud with commentary.

2 DICKASON, DAVID. "Henry Adams and Clarence King: The Record of a Friendship." New England Quarterly, 17 (June), 229-54.

Preliminary account of King's biography and of his relationship with Henry Adams.

1945 A BOOKS - NONE

1945 B SHORTER WRITINGS

1 BAYM, MAX I. "Henry Adams and the Critics." American Scholar, 15 (Winter 1945-46), 79-89.
Argues against taking Henry Adams's literary self-portrait as a "failure" too seriously.

2 BURKE, KENNETH. A Grammar of Motives. New York: Prentice Hall, passim.
Earlier version of 1962.B3, which comments more fully on the work of Henry Adams.

3 CHRISTY, ARTHUR E. "The Sense of the Past," in The Asian Legacy and American Life. Edited by Arthur E. Christy. New York: John Day Co., pp. 43-45.
Brief account of Henry Adams's interest in Asia and in Edwin Arnold's Light of Asia (1879). Reprinted: 1968.B3.

4 HUME, ROBERT A. "The Style and Literary Background of Henry Adams." American Literature, 16 (January), 296-315.
Written "with attention to The Education of Henry Adams," in which the style is similar to Sherwood Anderson's A Story Teller's Story (1924). Traces influences on Adams, including family, reading, editing, and literary ideals.

5 SILVER, ARTHUR W. "Henry Adams' 'Diary of a Visit to Manchester.'" American Historical Review, 51 (October), 74-89.
Reprints the essay with an account of Henry Adams's life during 1861, when it was written and first printed. Bibliographical details and some consideration of the mixed critical reception in England and America.

6 WRIGHT, NATHALIA. "Henry Adams's Theory of History: A Puritan Defence." New England Quarterly, 18 (June), 204-10.
Henry Adams was aware of his own "Puritan caste of mind" but did not sufficiently acknowledge the moral activity of his intellect. So he deceived himself in the formulation of his "dynamic theory of history."

1946

1946 A BOOKS - NONE

1946 B SHORTER WRITINGS

1 QUINLIVAN, FRANCES. "Irregularities of the Mental Mirror." _Catholic World_, 163 (April), 58-65.
"Adams cannot be typed"; therefore, "one cannot resist the temptation to try to find a sequence of lights which may explain Adams. . . ." Concentrates on Henry Adams's religious "lights."

1947 A BOOKS - NONE

1947 B SHORTER WRITINGS

1 AIKEN, CONRAD. _The Kid_ (poem). New York: Duell Sloan and Pearce.
Section 8, "The Last Vision," pays tribute to Henry Adams's search for "godhead" during the dark journey of his life.

2 CATER, HAROLD DEAN. "Biographical Introduction" to _Henry Adams and His Friends: A Collection of His Unpublished Letters_. Edited by Harold Dean Cater. Boston: Houghton Mifflin, pp. xv-cvii.
Account of life and work based on new material found in the letters which follow. "Appendix," pp. 781-784, prints for the first time Henry Adams's letter meant to accompany "The Rule of Phase Applied to History," and linking that essay to _The Education of Henry Adams_.

3 _____. "Henry Adams Reports on a German Gymnasium." _American Historical Review_, 53 (October), 59-74.
Prints unpublished early essay (1859) of Henry Adams on German education, with editorial comment.

4 HYMAN, STANLEY EDGAR. _The Armed Vision_. New York: Knopf, passim.
Attempts to "correct" Yvor Winters and other critics of Henry Adams's writings. Reprinted: 1955.B7.

5 MADISON, CHARLES A. _Critics and Crusaders: A Century of American Protest_. New York: Henry Holt and Co., pp. 285-307.
Asserts that Brooks Adams influenced Henry Adams's later writings.

6 MILLER, RICHARD F. "Henry Adams and the Influence of Women." American Literature, 18 (January), 291-98.
Neither heroine (Democracy or Esther) "can be convinced by reason" alone; both fail to find the necessary faith, and each novel ends inconclusively. Also cites "Primitive Rights of Women," Chartres, and the Education.

7 RAHV, PHILIP. Discovery of Europe: The Story of American Experience in the Old World. Boston: Houghton Mifflin Co., p. 332.
Headnote to selections from Henry Adams's letters from Europe. Contrasts his attitudes with those of Henry James.

8 SPILLER, ROBERT E. "Introduction" to Travels: Tahiti. New York: Scholar's Facsimiles and Reprints.
Reprint of Memoirs of Marau Taaroa Last Queen of Tahiti (1893): "only two copies seem now to exist."

9 WINTERS, YVOR. In Defense of Reason. Chicago: Swallow Press.
Reprint of 1938.B5; 1943.B5.

1948 A BOOKS

1 SAMUELS, ERNEST. The Young Henry Adams. Life and Writings 1838-1877. Cambridge, Massachusetts: Harvard University Press.
First volume of the three-volume biography (see 1958.A1 and 1964.A1). Intended to correct the misrepresentations of the Education throughout the three volumes. Draws on published and unpublished letters and Adams Papers. General goal of biographer: "a coherent body of fact with a modicum of interpretation."

1948 B SHORTER WRITINGS

1 AGAR, HERBERT. "Introduction," in The Formative Years: A History of the United States During the Administrations of Jefferson and Madison. Condensed and edited by Herbert Agar. 2 Vols. London: Collins.
Brief analysis of History in terms of important themes: family, party, American sectionalism, internationalism, the study of individuals, the Providential plan.

2 GLICKSBERG, CHARLES I. "Henry Adams the Journalist." New England Quarterly, 21 (June), 232-36.

1948

Between October 1868 and October 1870, Henry Adams contributed to the New York *Nation* and *Evening Post*. He authored "A Delicate Suggestion" (here reprinted), an editorial in the *Post* for 2 February 1870.

3 SHOEMAKER, RICHARD L. "The France of Henry Adams." *French Review*, 21 (February), 292-99.
Based on Adams's letters. Surveys changes in the author's attitudes.

4 SPILLER, ROBERT. "Henry Adams," in *Literary History of the United States*. Edited by Robert Spiller, et al. New York: Macmillan, pp. 1080-1103.
Often reprinted, pioneer account of Henry Adams's work as "a man of letters"; a mixture of biography and criticism. Reprinted: 1968.B18.

1949 A BOOKS - NONE

1949 B SHORTER WRITINGS

1 EDWARDS, HERBERT. "Henry Adams: Politician and Statesman." *New England Quarterly*, 22 (March), 49-60.
"There is little doubt that Henry Adams, despite his frequent disclaimers, longed most of his life for a position of power in politics." Traces this quest for power through Adams's life and writings, including letters.

2 LYDENBERG, JOHN. "Henry Adams and Lincoln Steffens." *South Atlantic Quarterly*, 48 (January), 42-64.
Compares the *Education* with Steffens's *Autobiography*, suggesting Adams's close relationship to literary naturalism.

1950 A BOOKS - NONE

1950 B SHORTER WRITINGS

1 BALDENSPERGER, FERNAND and WERNER P. FRIEDERICH. *Bibliography of Comparative Literature*. Chapel Hill: University of North Carolina Studies in Comparative Literature, p. 530.
Limited coverage now outdated; no index.

2 BEATTY, RICHMOND C. "Henry Adams and American Democracy." *Georgia Review*, 4 (Fall), 147-56.

Concentrates on Democracy to study expressions of Henry Adams's disenchantment with the course of politics and government in his time.

3 BURKE, KENNETH. A Rhetoric of Motives. New York: Prentice Hall.
Earlier version of 1962.B3, which comments more fully on the work of Henry Adams.

4 HESS, M. WHITCOMB. "Lin Yutang on Henry Adams." America, 84 (7 October), 16-18.
Considers Yutang's "case against Henry Adams" based upon an interpretation of "Prayer to the Virgin of Chartres." Sees Yutang "totally disregarding" Adams's intention in the poem by making Adams into a "materialist."

5 LÜDEKE, HENRY. "The Democracy of Henry Adams," in The 'Democracy' of Henry Adams and Other Essays. Swiss Studies in English, 24:23-77.
Foreign point of view on Henry Adams's attitudes toward political practices in America. Acknowledges that Adams used living politicians as models for his characters.

6 PAGE, EVELYN. "'The Man Around the Corner': An Episode in the Career of Henry Adams." New England Quarterly, 23 (September), 401-403.
Attributes to Charles Francis Adams, Jr. the "unfavorable review" of Gallatin that appeared in two issues of the Nation in August, 1879. See 1879.B1, B2.

7 ROELOFS, GERRIT H. "Henry Adams: Pessimism and the Intelligent Use of Doom." Journal of English Literary History, 17 (September), 214-39.
Treats Chartres, the Education, "Rule of Phase Applied to History," and "A Letter to American Teachers of History" as their author's unitary statement of pessimism.

8 SEIDENBERG, RODERICK. Posthistoric Man: An Inquiry. Chapel Hill: University of North Carolina Press, pp. 114-124, 234-35.
Argues the importance of Henry Adams's ideas concerning "Historic Determinism." Although Adams "approached the problem from the wrong end," his thesis may lead to "a new approach," and "the question Adams raised in the domain of history . . . must be accepted as valid, if unanswered."

9 TAYLOR, WILLIAM R. "Historical Bifocals on the Year 1800." New England Quarterly, 23 (June), 172-86.

Compares and contrasts Henry Adams's opening chapters of the History with John B. McMaster's A History of the People of the U. S. (1885) to demonstrate Adams's regional New England bias in the entire History.

1951 A BOOKS

1 BAYM, MAX I. The French Education of Henry Adams. New York: Columbia University Press.

Extended survey of Henry Adams's indebtedness to French philosophy, history, poetry, prose, and drama. Appendices include lists of Adams's French sources: "Philological Items," "Historical Items," "Tahiti Items in the Adams Collection" (many written in French), and Adams's marginalia in his edition of Descartes. Reprinted: 1969.A1.

2 HUME, ROBERT. Runaway Star: An Appreciation of Henry Adams. Ithaca: Cornell University Press.

Bibliography includes a list of "works containing letters of Henry Adams" (pp. 250-252) and "Appendix" prints "Prayer to the Virgin of Chartres" (pp. 239-244). Identifies three levels in "the sensibility of Henry Adams" which allowed for the achievements that establish his proper place as "an undoubted major figure in letters" (p. 231). Surveys all works including "collected letters . . . the best this country can show" (p. 231). As an artist, Henry Adams remains "a symbol of the tragic valor possible to man as he fronts infinity and finds it void of all certain promise but his own" (p. 238).

1951 B SHORTER WRITINGS

1 AARON, DANIEL. Men of Good Hope. New York: Oxford University Press, pp. 276-80.

Studies relationship between Henry Adams and Brooks Adams.

2 ANDERSON, THORNTON. Brooks Adams, Constructive Conservative. Ithaca: Cornell University Press, passim.

Relationship of the brothers Adams with special attention to unpublished letters between Henry Adams and Brooks Adams.

3 ARVIN, NEWTON. "Introduction" to The Selected Letters of Henry Adams. Edited by Newton Arvin. New York: Farrar, Straus and Young, pp. ix-xxx.

Surveys this selection of previously published letters, which represent mostly "the letter as a serious literary form," and Henry Adams's fourth-generation extension of a family habit. " . . . the letters enable one to follow the development of his mind from phase to phase."

4 GLICKSBERG, CHARLES I. "Henry Adams and the Aesthetic Quest." Prairie Schooner, 25:241-50.
Brief biographical survey of Henry Adams's development as a writer.

5 GOHDES, CLARENCE. "Late Nineteenth Century," in The Literature of the American People. Edited by A. H. Quinn. New York: Appleton-Century-Crofts, pp. 782-89.
Henry Adams treated largely as a historian who inherited Parkman's "mood of ironic pessimism." Yet his interest in science remains "remarkable" for a literary mind; overall "he is the most fascinating literary figure of his times."

6 GREENLEAF, RICHARD. "History, Marxism, and Henry Adams." Science and Society, 15 (Summer), 193-208.
Although Henry Adams and Karl Marx never met, Marxism "haunted Adams's 'intellectual life.'" "Marxism fascinated him, but he feared it" and unlike Twain and Crane, never escaped the chains of an "impure materialism."

7 HESS, M. WHITCOMB. "The Atomic Age and Henry Adams." Catholic World, 172:256-63.
Finds that Henry Adams "remains an enigma to many of us today" because he was both an "intellectual non-conformist" and a "spiritual non-conformist." Stresses Adams's dark prophetic insights into modern history, which he expressed alongside a personal devotion to "the Mother of Christ."

8 KIRK, RUSSELL. John Randolph of Roanoke: A Study in Conservative Thought. Chicago: University of Chicago Press, passim.
Acknowledges Conservatives' debt to Henry Adams's John Randolph, History, and Writings of Albert Gallatin. Reprinted: 1964.B5.

9 SCHRIFTGIESSER, KARL. The Lobbyists: The Art and Business of Influencing Lawmakers. Boston: Little, Brown, and Co., p. 15.
Concentrates on Henry Adams's activities as "amateur" lobbyist during his residence in Washington.

10 WASSER, HENRY. "The Thought of Henry Adams." New England Quarterly, 24 (December), 495-509.
Claims a priority for Henry Adams's scientific, over historical or artistic, thinking; the "Rule of Phase" represents a grander achievement than the Education.

1952 A BOOKS

1 JORDY, WILLIAM H. Henry Adams: Scientific Historian. New Haven and London: Yale University Press.
Considers Henry Adams's lifelong relationship to science and scientific thought, especially as revealed in essays, History, and the Education. Finds Adams to be an amateur in science, lacking "professionalism." Nevertheless, his "awareness of literary value . . . saved Adams from a blind faith in science." "Selected Bibliography" (pp. 291-317) considers special topics relevant to Adams's thought and life. Reprinted: 1963.A1.

1952 B SHORTER WRITINGS

1 ANON. Review of 1952 reprint of Democracy. New Yorker (23 August), p. 77.
"A strutting, graciously phrased little novel of Washington society in the eighteen-seventies."

2 BLACKMUR, R. P. "The Atlantic Unities." Hudson Review, 5 (Summer), 212-32.
Reviews Henry Adams's longtime interest in Russia, the political force that he acknowledged as the power of the future in the Education, and relates his ideas to "his vision of foreign affairs." Overall, "Adams had the luck and the vitality of imagination to see a great deal," and thus to be an accurate prophet of events to come. Refers to unpublished letters of Henry Adams. Finally, "The light into which Adams brings the necessity of a world policy is not the light of statesmanship but the light of criticism. . . . It corrected the present by looking to the future, and by feeling the shift of the forces of the past."

3 _____. "The Harmony of True Liberalism: Henry Adams' Mont-Saint-Michel and Chartres." Sewanee Review, 60 (Winter), 1-27.
Concentrates on Henry Adams's concern for faith and work as necessary parts of "unity" in human thought and life. Reprinted: 1967.B4.

6 WAGNER, VERN. "The Lotus of Henry Adams." New England Quarterly, 27 (March), 75-94.
Preliminary consideration of Henry Adams's method and importance. Developed further in 1969.A2.

1955 A BOOKS - NONE

1955 B SHORTER WRITINGS

1 BERINGAUSE, ARTHUR F. Brooks Adams: A Biography. New York: Knopf, passim.
Closely studies the mutual influence of the two brothers, especially to locate in Brooks's Law of Civilization and Decay the evidence of Henry's "hatred of commonality and his love for religion as a unifying force" (pp. 4-5).

2 BLACKMUR, R. P. "Adams Goes to School." Kenyon Review, 17 (Autumn), 597-623.
A "highly simplified account with an even more simplified explanation" of what Henry Adams professed to have learned from his life. Concentrates on the material in the Education, noting "Adams' experience and insight were much like those of the Puritans as described by Perry Miller, . . . but his means of coming to terms--his operative incentives--were very different." Some attention to Chartres, Democracy, and Esther, which also demonstrate his attempts "to make types and symbols in permanent form."

3 _____. The Lion and the Honeycomb. New York: Harcourt, Brace, pp. 79-96.
Reprints 1936.B1.

4 BLANCK, JACOB. "Henry Brooks Adams: 1838-1918," in Bibliography of American Literature. New Haven: Yale University Press, Vol. 1, pp. 1-11.
Descriptive bibliography of separately published works (not articles). Also reprints "Syllabus: History II: Political History of Europe From the 10th to the 15th Century," from a course Adams taught at Harvard College (p. 2).

5 CLARK, HARRY HAYDEN. "Influence of Science on American Literary Criticism." Transactions of the Wisconsin Academy of Arts and Sciences, 44:162f.
Briefly examines Chartres and the Education to document the general debt that Henry Adams owed to Hippolyte Taine. See also 1951.A1.

1955

6 COOKE, J. E. "Chats with Henry Adams." American Heritage, 7 (December), 42-45.
Frederic Bancroft, "biographer and historian of the South," recorded these remarks of Henry Adams after conversations with him.

7 HYMAN, STANLEY EDGAR. The Armed Vision. New York: Vintage.
Reprint of 1947.B4.

8 PERKINS, DEXTER. "Prefatory Note," in The United States in 1800. Ithaca, New York: Cornell University Press, pp. v-vi.
" . . . the six chapters reveal fine historical sweep and genuine penetration" (p. vi).

9 _____. "Henry Adams, A Biographical Note," in The United States in 1800. Ithaca, New York: Cornell University Press, pp. ix-x.

10 PREUSCHEN, KARL A. Das Problem der "Unity" und "Multiplicity" in seiner literarischen Gestaltung bei Henry Adams. Heidelberg: Carl Winter.
Treats a significant theme in Henry Adams's thought and writing, especially in poetry, Chartres, and the Education.

11 ROSSITER, CLINTON. Conservatism in America. New York: Knopf, pp. 156-62.
Sees Henry Adams as a dissenting conservative in an age of industrial expansion but still an important heir of the Conservative tradition established by "his great-grandfather John."

1956 A BOOKS

1 STEVENSON, ELIZABETH. Henry Adams: A Biography. New York: Macmillan.
Concentrates on Henry Adams as both skillful author and artist's subject in the Education. The portrait emerges as that of a "Satanic gentleman," very charming and most at home in his "private world of women." Reprinted: 1961.A2.

2 WASSER, HENRY. The Scientific Thought of Henry Adams. Thessaloniki, Greece: (Privately printed).
An account of Henry Adams's scientific interest and development as amateur scientist. Includes some of Adams's marginalia.

1956 B SHORTER WRITINGS

1 BERTHOFF, WARNER B. and DAVID BONNELL GREEN. "Henry Adams and Wayne MacVeagh." Pennsylvania Magazine of History and Biography, 80:493-512.

Prints "Hitherto unpublished letters" from Adams to MacVeagh with brief editorial remarks.

2 BUTTERFIELD, L. H. "The Papers of the Adams Family: Some Account of their History." Proceedings of the Massachusetts Historical Society, 71 (1953-57), 329-56.

Includes consideration of Henry Adams's contributions to the Adams Papers.

3 ELIAS, ROBERT H. "Prefatory Note," in Chapters of Erie. Ithaca, New York: Cornell University Press, pp. v-viii.

In these neglected essays, Henry Adams and his brother Charles, "perceived and illuminated with philosophical insight and felicitous artistry the character of the American nation and its essentially dialectic development" (p. vi).

4 KARIEL, HENRY S. "The Limits of Social Science: Henry Adams' Quest for Order." American Political Science Review, 50 (December), 1074-92.

Henry Adams anticipated much of the significant work in modern social science; yet he did not restrain himself from "pushing" his ideas to unwarranted conclusions. His tone was "profoundly anti-humanistic," although he always affirmed "good form."

5 SAVETH, EDWARD N. "The Heroines of Henry Adams." American Quarterly, 8 (Fall), 231-42.

Traces "ambivalence" in Henry Adams's feelings toward women, which shows up in his novels and other works, at times as "a theory of feminine superiority." All his "heroines" are versions of a feminine "prototype" who is both strong and destructive.

6 SCHEVILL, FERDINAND. "Henry Adams' Achievement and Defeat." Six Historians. Chicago: University of Chicago Press, pp. 157-90.

Divides Henry Adams's career into four stages and includes discussion of key works. Chartres rated above History, as the "most penetrating book on the medieval spirit ever produced by an American."

7 SCHEYER, ERNST. "The Adams Memorial by Augustus Saint-Gaudens." Art Quarterly, 19 (Summer), 178-97.

Brief account of the origins and importance in Adams's thought of the sculptor's work. Revised and expanded in 1970.A3.

8 TRILLING, LIONEL. "Adams at Ease," in A Gathering of Fugitives. Boston: Beacon Press, pp. 117-24.

Considers selection of Henry Adams's letters (Arvin ed.) and a reprint of Democracy. " . . . we shall do ourselves a great disservice, if ever we try to read Adams permanently out of our intellectual life." Reprinted from The Griffin (1952).

9 VALENTINE, ALAN. Trial Balance: The Education of an American. New York: Pantheon Books, pp. 7-10, 260-77, and passim.

An autobiography which attempts "to trace the effects of twentieth-century forces on a man trained for the nineteenth." The author "was attracted by the idea of carrying forward the story of the education of an American from the point where Henry Adams left off."

1957 A BOOKS

1 LEVENSON, J. C. The Mind and Art of Henry Adams. Boston: Houghton Mifflin.

Comprehensive study of Henry Adams's thought and writings. Treats the subject chronologically, considering influences on and development of Adams's philosophy and artistry. All major works receive attention, and focus remains on the literary techniques throughout. "While earlier Adamses wrote as public men even in their private correspondence, Henry Adams wrote as a private citizen, whether he was a private secretary or a professorial scholar who put his work before so limited an audience that publication served to conceal" (p. 23). Reprinted: 1968.A1.

1957 B SHORTER WRITINGS

1 BONNER, THOMAS N. "Henry Adams: A Sketch and an Analysis." Historian, 20 (November), 58-79.

Considers the comparative values of Adams's life and writings, especially the Education: "He is the one important American historian whose life is more significant than the history he wrote."

2 POCHMANN, HENRY A. German Culture in America. Madison: University of Wisconsin Press, passim.
Studies influences of German historical training, thought, and literature on Henry Adams, especially as shown in the Education.

3 SAVETH, EDWARD N. "Henry Adams: Waning of America's Patriciate: A Conservative's Destructive Impulses." Commentary, 24 (October), 302-309.
Traces Adams's views as prophet and his career as representative of declining fortunes of his class and family.

4 TAYLOR, FRANCIS HENRY. "Introduction" to Mont-Saint-Michel and Chartres. New York: The Heritage Press [Also, Limited Editions Club], pp. vii-xiii.
Finds Chartres "much less fact than fiction," yet "a literary masterpiece which will long outlive the widely divergent scholarly researches of which it is composed." Relies on letters to show that Adams "read into this age the peculiar problems of his private experience and of his imagination."

5 WALTERS, RAYMOND, JR. Albert Gallatin: Jeffersonian Financier and Diplomat. New York: Macmillan, passim.
Assesses the achievement of Henry Adams in his Albert Gallatin, finding the same "scholarly care" but little of the "literary skill" of the History. His subject was presented "very much in his own Boston Brahmin image" (p. vii).

1958 A BOOKS

1 SAMUELS, ERNEST. Henry Adams: The Middle Years. Life and Writings 1878-1891. Cambridge, Massachusetts: Harvard University Press.
Second volume of the three volume biography (see 1948.A1 and 1964.A1). Considerable attention to the circumstances surrounding the composition of Gallatin, Randolph, Democracy, Esther, and the History.

1958 B SHORTER WRITINGS

1 CAIRNS, JOHN C. "The Successful Quest of Henry Adams." South Atlantic Quarterly, 57 (Spring), 168-93.
If Henry Adams's lifelong intellectual "quest" had any meaning, "it was expressed in the acceptance of the relativity of all historical interpretation, the tentativeness of all understanding."

1958

2 CHASE, RICHARD. *The Democratic Vista: A Dialogue on Life and Letters in Contemporary America*. Garden City: Doubleday and Co., passim.

Treats Henry Adams's ideas (esp. *Chartres*) in the form of fictional dialogue.

3 GROSS, HARVEY. "'Gerontion' and the Meaning of History." *PMLA*, 73 (June), 299-304.

Studies the relationship between T. S. Eliot and Henry Adams. More fully developed in 1971.B5.

4 HAYWARD, IRA N. "From Tahiti to Chartres: The Henry Adams-John La Farge Friendship." *Huntington Library Quarterly*, 21 (August), 345-58.

Describes Huntington Library copy of *Tahiti* (1893) and gives details of the friendship.

5 HOCHFIELD, GEORGE. "Introduction" to *The Great Secession Winter of 1860-61 and Other Essays by Henry Adams*. Edited by George Hochfield. New York: Sagamore Press, pp. xi-xx.

Treats essays "as a single, related body of work"--"the first distinct phase of Henry Adams's literary career" (p. xi). Sees Henry Adams's political criticism contained here as determined by "assumptions . . . derived from his family background" (p. xiii), especially "the question of right and wrong" (p. xiv) and the question "of the Constitution" (p. xiv).

6 MAUD, RALPH. "Henry Adams: Irony and Impasse." *Essays in Criticism*, 8 (October), 381-92.

Focuses attention on irony, metaphor and "symbol-making." The reader should always ask what Henry Adams is trying to say at a level of "non-ironic seriousness."

7 McCORMICK, JOHN. "Henry Adams' *Democracy* Reconsidered." *Zur Geschichte und Problematik der Demokratie: Festgabe für Hans Herzfeld*. Edited by William Berges and Carl Henrichs. Berlin: Duncker and Hamblot, pp. 639-50.

Argues on grounds of style, technique, and idea that *Democracy* should "rank highly among minor, lasting novels of the nineteenth century."

8 STEVENSON, ELIZABETH. "Introduction" to *A Henry Adams Reader*. Edited by Elizabeth Stevenson. Garden City, New York: Doubleday, pp. ix-xvi.

Selections from prose and poetry are introduced with a brief biographical account.

9 WHITE, LYNN, JR. "Dynamo and Virgin Reconsidered." American Scholar, 27 (Spring), 183-94.
Summarizes Henry Adams's knowledge of medieval history to demonstrate that Chapter XXV of the Education does not discuss symbolic polarities. Reprinted: 1969.B15.

10 WILKINS, THURMAN. Clarence King: A Biography. New York: Macmillan, passim.
Treats King's influence on Henry Adams's life and writings, including the impact of geological thought.

1959 A BOOKS - NONE

1959 B SHORTER WRITINGS

1 BARRETT, C. WALLER. "The Making of a History: Letters of Henry Adams to Henry Vignaud and Charles Scribner, 1879-1913." Proceedings of the Massachusetts Historical Society, 71:204-71.
Prints 55 letters with brief editorial commentary.

2 BAYM, MAX I. "Three Moths and a Candle: A Study of the Impact of Pascal on Walter Pater, Henry Adams and Wallace Stevens." Comparative Literature: Proceedings of the Second Congress on the International Comparative Literature Association (University of North Carolina Studies in Comparative Literature, Vol. 2, no. 24). Edited by Werner P. Friederich, Chapel Hill, N. C., 2:336-48.
Traces influence of Pascal on Adams, pp. 340-45.

3 DAVIES, WALLACE EVAN. "Religious Issues in Late Nineteenth-Century American Novels." Bulletin of the John Rylands Library, 41 (March), 328-59.
Finds Henry Adams's religious skepticism "complete" because science appears no more helpful than religion in his writings.

4 FABIAN, BERNHARD. "Henry Adams: Ein Forschungsbericht 1918-1958." Archiv für Kulturgeschichte, 41:218-59.
Bibliography with citations in English; not always reliable.

5 MacLEAN, KENNETH. "Window and Cross in Henry Adams' Education." University of Toronto Quarterly, 28 (July), 332-44.
Studies symbols and images, with suggestions for possible meanings.

1959

6 MILLER, JAMES E., JR. "Walt Whitman and the Secret of History." Centennial Review, 3 (Summer), 320-36.
Studies Henry Adams's response to Whitman in the context of a common sense of "history."

7 MUNFORD, HOWARD M. "Henry Adams and the Tendency of History." New England Quarterly, 23 (March), 79-90.
Seeks to correct other views of Henry Adams's philosophy of history (as expressed in late essays) by pointing to "grim humor" and "elaborate irony," which make "scientific history" something of a joke.

8 PREUSCHEN, KARL. "Henry Adams (1838-1918): Zur Kontinuität in seinem literarischen Schaffen." Jahrbuch für Amerika-Studien, 4:52-63.
Surveys Adams's major writings (including some essays) with special attention to political and social views.

9 RICHIE, DONALD. "Henry Adams in Japan." Japan Quarterly, 6 (October-December), 434-42.
Reviews evidence in Henry Adams's writings and concludes that he did not understand Japan or the Japanese.

10 SAVETH, EDWARD N. "The Middle Years of Henry Adams: Women in His Life and Novels." Commentary, 27 (May), 429-33.
Faults Ernest Samuels (Henry Adams: The Middle Years) for lack of "imaginativeness" in dealing with Elizabeth Cameron and with the "emotional life" of Henry Adams in general. Calls attention to Adams's "penchant for the strong destructive woman."

11 STEIN, WILLIAM. "The Portrait of a Lady: Vis Inertiae." Western Humanities Review, 13 (Spring), 177-90.
Briefly compares ideas of Henry Adams and Henry James about "the problem of American women which so absorbed Adams." Concentrates on the Education. Reprinted: 1967.B17.

12 WELLAND, D. S. R. "Henry Adams as Novelist." Renaissance and Modern Studies, 3:25-50.
Uses broad discussion of Adams's life to demonstrate the value of his novels: "It is very easy to underestimate Henry Adams as novelist," and English critics, in particular, have not done justice to his work.

13 WHITTEMORE, REED. "Mr. Tate and Mr. Adams." Sewanee Review, 67 (October-December), 582-84.
Sees Henry Adams as a representative of "Positivism."

1960 A BOOKS - NONE

1960 B SHORTER WRITINGS

1 BOROMÉ, JOSEPH A. "Henry Adams Silenced by the Cotton Famine." New England Quarterly, 33 (June), 237-40.
Prints unpublished early essay with brief commentary.

2 HESS, M. WHITCOMB. "The Enigma of Henry Adams." Contemporary Review, 197 (June), 325-28.
Uses Adams's poetry to document the "Christian" enigma in his life and thought.

3 KORETZ, GENE H. "Augustine's Confessions and The Education of Henry Adams." Comparative Literature, 12 (Summer), 193-206.
Studies literary influence of Augustine as pioneer autobiographer, who helped to shape the form and content of the Education.

4 LEVENSON, J. C. "Henry Adams and the Culture of Science," in Studies in American Culture. Edited by Joseph Kwiat and Mary Turpie. Minneapolis: University of Minnesota Press, pp. 123-28.
By the time Henry Adams came to write the Education "he was prepared to mock the religion of progress," especially scientific progress, but other forms of human progress as well. "Indeed, his capacity to fuse his most intimate suffering [following the death of his wife] and his most abstract deliberations is the mark of Adams's genius." Traces debt to W. James's Principles of Psychology.

5 PETERSON, MERRILL D. The Jeffersonian Image in the American Mind. New York: Oxford University Press, pp. 280-91 and passim.
Recognizes "popular influence" of Henry Adams's treatment in the History. Since its appearance, "no one has attempted to rewrite the history of the period and few, apparently, have felt the need to do so." Reprinted: 1962.B14.

6 PRIESTLEY, J. B. Literature and Western Man. New York: Harper & Brothers, pp. 357-58.
Views Henry Adams as "an 'expatriate' from the whole modern age." Despite its faults of style, "the Education . . . is one of the best accounts we possess of a sensitive enquiring mind in the latter half of the nineteenth century." A brief biography also included (p. 447).

1960

7 SAMUELS, ERNEST. "Henry Adams' 20th Century Virgin." Christian Century, 77 (5 October), 1143-46.
Summarizes Henry Adams's religious views and their relationship to Roman Catholic theology, especially the "Marian development," and to the anthropology of his time.

8 WISH, HARVEY. The American Historian: A Social-Intellectual History of the Writing of the American Past. New York: Oxford University Press, pp. 158-80.
Studies Henry Adams's standing among "scientific historians" and surveys his critics and his other writings as well as the History.

9 WOODWARD, C. VANN. The Burden of Southern History. Baton Rouge: Louisiana State University Press, pp. 117-27, 134-40.
Relies on Democracy and the Education to measure Henry Adams's "ambivalent attitudes" toward the South.

1961 A BOOKS

1 DONOVAN, TIMOTHY PAUL. Henry Adams and Brooks Adams: The Education of Two American Historians. Norman, Oklahoma: University of Oklahoma Press.
Concentrates on family influences (from early generations as well as in Henry's) which affected the thought and writing of the two brothers. Henry was caught between a sense of history-as-drama and his skeptical response to the dramatic view. His approach to life and history became "oblique" rather than direct.

2 STEVENSON, ELIZABETH. Henry Adams: A Biography. New York: Collier Books.
Reprint of 1956.A1.

1961 B SHORTER WRITINGS

1 AIKEN, HENRY DAVID. "Foreword" to Democracy: An American Novel by Henry Adams. New York: Signet, pp. v-xii.
Cites J. C. Levenson's Mind and Art of Henry Adams and emphasizes "the complexity of the moral issues" in Democracy and "Adams's skillful handling of the complex ambiguities implicit in the relationship between Ratcliffe and Mrs. Lee."

2 CANTOR, MILTON. "Introduction" to John Randolph by Henry Adams. Greenwich, Conn.: Fawcett, pp. vii-xv.

Reviews Henry Adams's attitudes toward Randolph and explains "the unevenness of the biography."

3 MOONEY, STEPHEN. "The Education of Henry Adams (Poet)." Tennessee Studies in Literature, 6:25-32.
During his career as a prose writer, Henry Adams "always displayed the imagistic imagination of a poet." Studies examples of his poetry.

4 SAMUELS, ERNEST. "Introduction" to Democracy and Esther. Combined Edition. Garden City, N. Y.: Anchor Books, Doubleday and Co., pp. ix-xix.
Treats Democracy as the work of "an instinctive satirist," and Esther as "an anticipation" of Henry Adams's "major themes" in the later writing.

*5 TAKUWA, SHINJI. "Some Impressions of Henry Adams, Hart Crane, E. E. Cummings, and Others." Studies in English Literature and Language (Kyushu University, Japan), 11:19-53.
Unlocatable; cited in 1969.B13.

6 TANNER, TONY. "The Lost America--The Despair of Henry Adams and Mark Twain." Modern Age, 5 (Summer), 299-310.
The theme of despair is common to both writers in their "late works," written when they were confronted by "the machine and the mob." Twain's "vision of life as chaos is, in essence and conclusion, not very different from that of Henry Adams" in the Education, as the "recurrent imagery" reveals. Reprinted: 1963.B11.

1962 A BOOKS

1 HOCHFIELD, GEORGE. Henry Adams: An Introduction and Interpretation. New York: Barnes and Noble. American Authors and Critics Series.
Provides an introduction to all of Henry Adams's writings; includes: critical consideration, a chronology of his life, and a "Selected Bibliography." Reprinted: 1967.A1.

1962 B SHORTER WRITINGS

1 BELL, MILLICENT. "Adams' Esther: The Morality of Taste." New England Quarterly, 35 (June), 147-61.
Adams lacked a "sense of vocation" as a novelist and Esther is "too personal, too private" to be considered

1962

anything except "coterie literature," written for "a private group of friends." The reader must supply "some sort of annotation from the record of Adams' life."

2 BRUMM, URSULA. "Henry Adams als Historiker: Seine Bedeutung für die amerikanische Literatur und Geistesgeschichte." _Archiv für das Studium der neueren Sprachen und Literaturen_, 199 (October), 209-28.

Surveys Henry Adams's thought and places him with Whitman and others in an optimistic tradition.

3 BURKE, KENNETH. _A Grammar of Motives and Rhetoric of Motives_ (combined edition). Cleveland and New York: Meridian Books, World Publishing Co., passim.

Studies rituals and symbols in Henry Adams's work, especially the _Education_, which "seems to be a rebirth ritual" (p. 120). The Virgin and the dynamo show a "contrast between the natural powers and the industrial powers." Revised reprinting of 1945.B2 and 1950.B3.

4 COVICI, PASCAL, JR. _Mark Twain's Humor: The Image of a World_. Dallas: Southern Methodist University Press, pp. 134-39.

"Adams's method of dealing with forces suddenly turned chaotic is a helpful point of comparison from which to examine Twain's response." Based chiefly on _Chartres_ and the _Education_.

5 ELIOT, T. S. "A Sceptical Patrician," in _Major Writers of America_. Vol. II. Edited by Perry Miller. New York: Harcourt, Brace & World, pp. 793-96.

Reprint of 1919.B2.

6 FIEDLER, LESLIE. _Love and Death in the American Novel_. Revised Edition. Cleveland and New York: Dell Publishing Co., passim.

Considering _Democracy_ and _Esther_, Henry Adams "cannot imagine a truly sexual heroine." Instead, he "insisted upon imposing that divine ideal on actual ladies whom he knew" (pp. 276-77). Reprinted: 1966.B6.

7 GREIFER, ELISHA. "The Conservative Pose in America: The Adamses' Search for a Pre-Liberal Past." _Western Political Quarterly_, 15 (March), 5-16 (esp. 9-13).

Fits Henry Adams into a family pattern: "Philosophic doubt of democracy . . . frustrated by an inability to free themselves from their stake in American life, not merely as bondholders, but more inescapably as inheritors of the liberal faith."

8 HOFSTADTER, RICHARD. Anti-Intellectualism in American Life. New York: Knopf, pp. 174-79 and passim.
Views Education as a political and intellectual testimonial of the genteel reformers. "Their towering literary monument proved to be that masterpiece in the artistry of self-pity, Henry Adams's Education."

9 KARITA, MOTOSHI. "Henry Adams in Japan." Studies in English Literature (Tokyo), pp. 133-53.
Despite the various forms of interest that Henry Adams showed in the country and its people, he was "unable to penetrate to the inner life of the Japanese."

10 McINTYRE, JOHN P. "Henry Adams and the Unity of Chartres." Twentieth Century Literature, 7 (January), 159-71.
The key to Adams's unity is found in the imaginative freedom the writer uses in treating history, philosophy, etc.

11 MUMFORD, LEWIS. "Apology to Henry Adams." Virginia Quarterly Review, 38 (Spring), 196-217.
A reappraisal of Henry Adams's value as a seer, emphasizing his view of modern history as a moral break-down.

12 PARK, FOSTER. "The German Education of Henry Adams." Appalachian State Teachers College Faculty Publications, pp. 35-46.
Studies German influences to conclude that they are important in understanding Adams.

13 PEARSON, NORMAN HOLMES. "Poetry and Language," in A Time of Harvest: American Literature, 1910-1960. Edited with an introduction by Robert Spiller. New York: Hill and Wang, pp. 65-72.
"The book which, more than any other, represents the American writer's entrance into the twentieth century is The Education of Henry Adams."

14 PETERSON, MERRILL D. The Jeffersonian Image in the American Mind. New York: Galaxy Books.
Reprint of 1960.B5.

15 RULE, HENRY B. "Henry Adams' Attack on Two Heroes of the Old South." American Quarterly, 14 (Summer), 174-84.

Cites "Captain John Smith" and *John Randolph* to prove that Henry Adams was a fourth-generation family voice in the anti-slavery campaign.

16 SAMUELS, ERNEST. "Henry Adams," in *Major Writers of America*. Vol. II. Edited by Perry Miller. New York: Harcourt, Brace & World, pp. 269-82.
Overview of Henry Adams's life and work, which emphasizes New England origins and tradition of dissent.

17 SCHEYER, ERNST. "The Aesthete Henry Adams." *Criticism*, 4 (Fall), 313-27.
Henry Adams's "theory of history was primarily aesthetically conditioned." Finds similarities with Kierkegaard. *See* 1970.A3.

18 WHITE, MORTON and LUCIA. "The Displaced Patrician," in *The Intellectual Versus the City: From Thomas Jefferson to Frank Lloyd Wright*. Cambridge, Massachusetts: Harvard University Press, pp. 54-74.
As "the displaced patrician," Henry Adams found fault with the city in *Democracy*, the *History*, and the *Education* not "in the name of nature" but "out of concern for civilization."

1963 A BOOKS

1 JORDY, WILLIAM H. *Henry Adams: Scientific Historian*. New Haven and London: Yale University Press.
New "Preface" (pp. vii-xiii) discusses recent scholarship on Henry Adams, published since 1952. Reprints 1952.A1.

1963 B SHORTER WRITINGS

1 DANGERFIELD, GEORGE and OTEY M. SCRUGGS. "Introduction" to Henry Adams's *History of the United States During the Administrations of Jefferson and Madison*. 2 Vols. Abridged and edited by Dangerfield and Scruggs. Englewood Cliffs, New Jersey: Prentice-Hall, pp. 1-10.
Discusses selected passages from the text of the abridgement.

2 FOLSOM, JAMES K. "Mutation as Metaphor in the *Education of Henry Adams*." *ELH*, 30 (June), 162-74.

Stresses non-literal treatment in Adams's story of his life, especially the "series of parallel metaphors dealing with the inexplicability of time," "geological" and "historic." The "three sentence conclusion" to the book shows that, as a "child of the X-Ray," twentieth-century man may be able to "think in complexities unimaginable to an earlier mind."

3 GLICKSBERG, CHARLES I. The Tragic Vision in Twentieth-Century Literature. Carbondale: Southern Illinois University Press, p. 169.
Note 8 relates Henry Adams's Education to "the modern tragic vision."

4 HAHN, HERBERT F. "The Education of Henry Adams Reconsidered." College English, 24 (March), 444-49.
Warns against overestimate of Henry Adams's "failure" caused by uncritical acceptance of the Education as truth.

5 LASKY, MELVIN J. "America and Europe: Transatlantic Images," in Paths of American Thought. Edited by Arthur M. Schlesinger, Jr. and Morton White. Boston: Houghton Mifflin Co., esp. pp. 479-83.
A glimpse of Adams as the pre-Spenglerian prophet of cultural decline.

6 MANE, ROBERT. "Henry Adams et la science." Etudes anglaises, 16 (January-March), 1-10.
Traces Adams's early interest in science to an apprehension of destructive possibilities.

7 PETERSON, MERRILL D. "Henry Adams on Jefferson the President." Virginia Quarterly Review, 39 (Spring), 187-201.
Quarrels with Adams's portrayal of Jefferson (in History) as a political failure.

8 RAYMOND, JOHN. "Henry Adams and the American Scene." History Today, 13 (May), 304-309.
Concise biography of Henry Adams; special attention to the Education and his experiences with politics and politicians. Part I of a two-part article. See 1963.B9.

9 _____. "Henry Adams and the American Scene." History Today, 13 (June), 390-97.
Part II of a two-part article. Continues and completes biographical account begun in 1963.B8.

1963

10 SAVETH, EDWARD N. "Introduction" to The Education of Henry Adams, in The Great Histories Series. Edited by Hugh R. Trevor-Roper. New York: Pocket Books, Washington Square, Ltd., pp. ix-xlvii.
Reviews Henry Adams's life and career, with special attention to his family, his interest in "force" as a key to history, and his anti-Semitism.

11 SMITH, HENRY NASH, ed. Mark Twain: A Collection of Critical Essays. Englewood Cliffs, New Jersey: Prentice Hall, pp. 159-74.
Reprints 1961.B6.

1964 A BOOKS

1 SAMUELS, ERNEST. Henry Adams: The Major Phase. Life and Writings, 1892-1918. Cambridge, Massachusetts: Harvard University Press.
Third volume of the three-volume biography (see 1948.A1 and 1958.A1). Appendix A outlines "The Travels of Henry Adams." And Appendix B completes the annotated bibliography of Henry Adams's writings (see all three volumes). Sticks to well documented conclusions concerning the subject's activities during this richest and most complicated period of his life. Little literary criticism is included.

1964 B SHORTER WRITINGS

1 BALTZELL, E. DIGBY. The Protestant Establishment: Aristocracy and Caste in America. New York: Random House, pp. 90-93.
Treats "Henry Adams: The Powerless Patrician" in terms of developing case of "anti-Semitism which eventually took hold of so brilliant a mind." Adams "embraced the idea of caste after losing faith in aristocracy."

2 FULLER, LOUISE FANT. "Henry Adams: Pilgrim to World's Fairs." Tennessee Studies in Literature, 9:1-10.
Studies Adams's responses to "the three fairs that he attended (1893 Columbian Exposition, 1895 at Chartres, 1900 Paris Exposition) and the effects on Chartres and the Education.

3 JAHER, FREDERIC COPLE. Doubters and Dissenters: Cataclysmic Thought in America, 1885-1918. Glencoe: Free Press, pp. 148-57.
Finds a family "pose" represented by Henry and Brooks Adams in the fourth generation. "Like his grandfather and

and great grandfather before him, retirement turned Henry into a disgruntled observer, both of himself and of the nation."

4 KAZIN, ALFRED. "Autobiography as Narrative." Michigan Quarterly Review, 3 (Fall), 210-16.

"There is great autobiography that is also intellectual history, like The Education of Henry Adams."

5 KIRK, RUSSELL. John Randolph of Roanoke: A Study in Conservative Thought. Chicago: Henry Regnery Co.

Reprint of 1951.B8.

6 MARX, LEO. The Machine in the Garden: Technology and the Pastoral Idea in America. New York: Oxford University Press, pp. 345-50.

"A sense of the transformation of life by technology dominates the Education as it does no other book." Adams represents the Manichean evaluation of American life, the "ultimate expressions of tragic doubleness . . . at the center of modern history."

7 PARSONS, LYNN HUDSON. "Continuing Crusade: Four Generations of the Adams Family View Alexander Hamilton." New England Quarterly, 37 (March), 43-63.

Applies the principle of family prejudice to Henry Adams's writing and editing, particularly in Documents Relating to New England Federalism and the History.

8 ROGAT, YOSAL. "Mr. Justice Holmes: Some Modern Views." University of Chicago Law Review, 31 (Winter), 213-56.

Adams, Henry James, and Holmes all shared a "preoccupation with the theme of the observer--the spectator--or in acting out that role," which shows up in their writings. With Holmes, in particular, Adams had in common both a special interest in "power" or "force" and a sense of ultimate helplessness that led to a desire for personal privacy.

9 SAYRE, ROBERT F. The Examined Self: Benjamin Franklin, Henry Adams, Henry James. Princeton: Princeton University Press, passim.

Labels the Education "epic autobiography," the outgrowth of "one of the boldest possible conceptions of autobiography" (p. 197). Comparison/contrast with Henry James, with some consideration of Franklin's literary influence. "The details of his theory of history do not concern the critic of Adams as an autobiographer" because Adams did not take theories "seriously" (p. 133).

1964

10 WILSON, LARMAN C. "Henry Adams and the Second Law of Thermodynamics." Texas Quarterly, 7 (Autumn), 29-33.
Adams found no satisfying answer to his quest for order in his use of the Second Law.

11 WIND, EDGAR. "The Long Battle Between Art and the Machine." Harper's Magazine, 228 (February), 65-72.
In the Education lies buried "one of the most enlightening of anti-mechanical protests. . . . On the side of art Adams disregarded the mechanical energies that had been harnessed to produce an admirable building, while on the side of mechanics, he considered energies in the raw, unrelated to any purposes they might subserve." Thus, in the Virgin-dynamo "antithesis," there are "mental omissions on both sides."

12 WINKS, ROBIN W. "Henry Adams' Philosophy of History." Dalhousie Review, 44 (Summer), 199-204.
Brief outline of Adams's thoughts on history.

1965 A BOOKS - NONE

1965 B SHORTER WRITINGS

1 ANDERSON, CHARLES. "Introduction" to Henry Adams, American Literary Masters. Vol. 2. New York: Holt, Rinehart, and Winston, pp. 317-42.
Identifies the "quest for form" as the "keynote" of Henry Adams's career as a writer. Both the Education and Chartres "aimed at discovering the meaning of history."

2 BERTHOFF, WARNER. The Ferment of Realism: American Literature, 1884-1919. New York: The Free Press, pp. 187-205.
Places Henry Adams among the "realists" who discovered that traditional literary forms "would not serve" their needs.

3 BREZINE, DON. "The Tragedy of Henry Adams." Crane Review, 8:18-31.
Traces the "tragedy" of Henry Adams as recounted in the Education and documented by the late essays, finding a key to definition in a double loss of "power": first, family (including personal) power in politics; second, "man in power" in the universe.

1965

4 BUCK, PAUL, et al. Social Sciences at Harvard, 1860-1920: From Inculcation to the Open Mind. Cambridge, Massachusetts: Harvard University Press, passim.
Various comments on Henry Adams's influence as a teacher at Harvard.

5 COLACURCIO, MICHAEL. "The Dynamo and the Angelic Doctor: The Bias of Henry Adams' Medievalism." American Quarterly, 17 (Winter), 696-712.
In Chartres, Adams shows how "reason inevitably destroys faith." Yet he always remained certain that personal conviction was necessary for human satisfaction.

6 DONOGHUE, DENIS. Connoisseurs of Chaos: Ideas of Order in Modern American Poetry. New York: Macmillan, pp. 9-22.
Uses Henry Adams, especially History, Chartres, and letters, as spokesman for the titular theme, applied to modern poetry.

7 GORDON, JOSEPH T. "The Gilded Age and Democracy: A Literary View of Post-Civil War America." The University of Houston Forum, 4 (Winter-Spring), 4-9.
Finds a "vast number of both accidental and substantial similarities" in plots and themes.

8 KAZIN, ALFRED. "Impressionist of Power." New York Review of Books, 3 (14 January), 6-7.
Reviews Samuels's Henry Adams: The Major Phase, with special attention to Adams's concern for "power, from a theoretical and philosophic point of view." Adams always "lacked some prime sense of himself as a power."

9 MacSHANE, FRANK. The American in Europe: A Collection of Impressions Written by Americans from the Seventeenth Century to the Present. Selected and edited by Frank MacShane. New York: E. P. Dutton and Co., pp. 183-84.
Headnote to selection from the Education claims that "Adams was the first American to consider the deeper meanings of European culture and its relationship to all of Western civilization."

10 MINDEL, JOSEPH. "The Uses of Metaphor: Henry Adams and the Symbols of Science." Journal of the History of Ideas, 26 (January-March), 89-102.
Uses modern scientific knowledge to correct Adams's scientific statements, claiming that Henry Adams failed to understand the "philosophy and methodology" of science.

1965

11 MONTEIRO, GEORGE. Henry James and John Hay: The Record of a Friendship. Providence: Brown University Press, pp. 136-37 and passim.

Many bits of information concerning Henry Adams's life as reported by his friends. Backgrounds of comments in the Education and elsewhere, especially in "Notes," pp. 147-87.

12 PIPER, HENRY DAN. F. Scott Fitzgerald: A Critical Portrait. Carbondale and Edwardsville: Southern Illinois University Press, pp. 44-47.

Traces the influence of Henry Adams and the Education on Fitzgerald.

13 RALEIGH, JOHN HENRY. The Plays of Eugene O'Neill. Carbondale: Southern Illinois University Press, pp. 246-51.

Compares the plays of O'Neill with Henry Adams's Education; finds two common themes: "the doubleness" of New England life and the preoccupation with "electrical force, the double power" (in the dynamo).

14 RULAND, RICHARD. "Tocqueville's De la démocratie en Amérique and The Education of Henry Adams." Comparative Literature Studies, 2:195-207.

Studies intellectual and literary influence to suggest parallels that enlarge the meaning of the Education.

15 SPILLER, ROBERT E. "After the Romantic Movement," in The Third Dimension: Studies in Literary History. New York: Macmillan Co., pp. 116-21.

First read before the American Literature Group of the Modern Language Association in December, 1947.

"Finally, the Education and the Chartres must themselves be defined in aesthetic terms . . . in the adequacy of their symbolism."

16 TRACHTENBERG, ALAN. Brooklyn Bridge: Fact and Symbol. New York: Oxford University Press, passim.

Concentrates on the Education to show that Henry Adams, as an observer of the politics of the gilded age, sought the kind of symbolic reconciliation of opposing forces which provides a key to the metaphoric significance of the bridge.

17 VITZTHUM, RICHARD C. "Henry Adams' Paraphrase of Sources in the History of the United States." American Quarterly, 17 (Spring), 81-91.

Studies "130 of the 190 published references" cited to demonstrate that "Adams derives the language and syntax of roughly a sixth of his own prose from that of his sources." Expanded in 1974.B17.

18 WHIPPLE, T. K. Spokesmen. Berkeley: University of California Press. Chapter on Henry Adams.
Reprints 1928.B2.

19 WILSON, LARMAN C. "The Degradation of the Democratic Dogma." New Mexico Quarterly, 35 (Autumn), 204-14.
Considers the "pessimism" of Brooks and Henry Adams, among other figures.

1966 A BOOKS - NONE

1966 B SHORTER WRITINGS

1 BLINDERMAN, ABRAHAM. "Henry Adams and the Jews." Chicago Jewish Forum, 25 (Fall), 3-8.
Relies on Adams's letters to document anti-Semitism in Adams's social views.

2 BLOTNER, JOSEPH. The Modern Political Novel: 1900-1960. Austin and London: University of Texas Press, pp. 110-11.
Democracy represents an important "predecessor . . . which set national politics in an atmosphere of moral sickness."

3 CAMPBELL, HARRY M. "Academic Criticism on Henry Adams: Confusion about Chaos." Midcontinent American Studies Journal, 7 (Spring), 3-14.
Seeks to correct earlier critics (especially Winters and Spiller) and to prove that Adams has been "both praised and condemned for the wrong reasons." His predictions foreshadow the modern "atheistic existentialists," such as Sartre and Camus.

4 COLACURCIO, MICHAEL. "Democracy and Esther: Henry Adams' Flirtation with Pragmatism." American Quarterly, 14 (Summer), 53-70.
The novels are "the clearest example" of Adams's understanding of pragmatism; they display "a very strong drive toward the practical, toward operation, toward power."

5 EDENBAUM, ROBERT I. "The Novels of Henry Adams: Why Man Failed." Texas Studies in Literature and Language, 8 (Summer), 245-55.

Democracy and *Esther* are both investigations of why men seemed to be failing in nineteenth-century life. Adams's heroines hold the key to finer sensibilities and to his sympathetic hope for something better.

6 FIEDLER, LESLIE. *Love and Death in the American Novel*. Revised Edition. Cleveland and New York: Dell Publishing Co.

Reprint of 1962.B6.

7 GREEN, MARTIN. *The Problem of Boston: Some Readings in Cultural History*. New York: W. W. Norton, pp. 142-62, 209-16.

Takes issue with Levenson's interpretation of Henry Adams's "power of mind" as a transcending artistic technique. Instead, Adams exemplified "a hatred of life." His is the problem of Boston.

8 GROSS, HARVEY. "History as Metaphysical Pathos: Modern Literature and the Idea of History." *Denver Quarterly*, 1 (Autumn), 1-22.

"Introductory chapter" to 1971.B5. Brooks and Henry Adams shared a special role in history: "we see them anticipating and confirming subsequent patterns of thought and feeling."

9 HOMANS, ABIGAIL ADAMS. "My Adams Uncles: Charles, Henry, Brooks." *Yale Review*, 55 (March), 321-46.

Personal reminiscence. Expanded in 1966.B10.

10 _____. *Education by Uncles*. Boston: Houghton Mifflin Co., passim.

"Adams Uncles" in the life of a young girl, especially Henry at home in Washington, D. C. Expanded version of 1966.B9.

11 LEVINE, PAUL. "A Conservative Christian Anarchist 19th Century Hipster." *Jubilee*, 13 (January), 48-49.

Reviews Samuels' *Major Phase* with special attention to Henry Adams's "anti-Semitism." " . . . I suspect that Adams's final appeal will be based less on his vision of the apocalypse than on his sense of the past."

12 LURIE, EDWARD. "American Scholarship: A Subjective Interpretation of Nineteenth-Century Cultural History," in *Essays on History and Literature*. Edited by Robert H. Bremner. Columbus: Ohio State University Press, pp. 31-80.

Henry Adams and his "elitist" friends exerted a special "cultural influence" on their time. He was "blinded" to the "sensibility" of Gibbs's science but not to the "intellectual and moral currents" in history and in life.

13 MADISON, CHARLES A. "Gleanings from the Henry Holt Files." _Princeton University Library Chronicle_, 27 (Winter), 86-106.

Provides details of publication of _Democracy_ and _Esther_, based on Henry Adams's correspondence with Holt.

14 MILNE, GORDON. _The American Political Novel_. Norman: University of Oklahoma Press, passim.

Chapter IV, "Expertise: Twain, De Forest, and Adams," cites _Democracy_ as "the most interesting of the post-Civil War political novels." Yet it remains a flawed achievement, "a novel _about_ things rather than an imaginative recreation of things."

15 SKOTHEIM, ROBERT ALLEN. _American Intellectual Histories and Historians_. Princeton: Princeton University Press, pp. 22-24 and passim.

Treats Henry Adams as a "scientific historian," who "raised the question of causal relationship between thought and its environment." The introduction and conclusion of the _History_ were "appended" to the core of political history; yet Adams "avowed great interest" in them by actually naming the concepts of "popular mind" and "national character" around which later history has been written.

16 WARREN, AUSTIN. _The New England Conscience_. Ann Arbor: University of Michigan Press, pp. 170-81.

"Adams' intellectual conscience, never extinguished by any amount of irony he poured on it, could scarcely be satisfied" by anything he wrote. Sees Henry Adams caught between being a "researcher" and an "interpreter."

17 ZIFF, LARZER. _The American 1890s: Life and Times of a Lost Generation_. New York: Viking Press, pp. 222-28.

Adams mentioned throughout; general influence summarized as that of an important representative intellectual of the period.

1967

1967 A BOOKS

1 HOCHFIELD, GEORGE. *Henry Adams: An Introduction and Interpretation*. New York: Holt, Rinehart, and Winston.
Reprint of 1962.A1.

1967 B SHORTER WRITINGS

1 ANDERSON, JOHN M. "The Source of Tragedy." *Phenomenology in America: Studies in the Philosophy of Experience*. Edited by James M. Edie. Chicago: Quadrangle Books, pp. 272-73.
The *Education* represents modern testimony of despair and tragedy.

2 ARVIN, NEWTON. *American Pantheon*. Edited by Daniel Aaron and L. Schendler. New York: Dell.
Pp. 199-221: "Letters of Henry Adams" reprinted from "Introduction" to *The Selected Letters of Henry Adams*.
Pp. 194-199 reprints: "A Warning; Not an Example," a review of the *Letters of Henry Adams, 1858-1891*. Edited by Worthington C. Ford.

3 BAYM, MAX I. "An Historian Prods a Philologist: The Letters of Henry Adams to William Dwight Whitney." *Yale University Library Gazette*, 42 (October), 77-101.
Previously unpublished letters of the 1870s, with substantial introduction.

4 BLACKMUR, R. P. *A Primer of Ignorance*. New York: Harcourt, Brace, and World.
Pp. 251-73: reprints 1940.B1, "Henry Adams: Three Late Moments."
Pp. 201-25: reprints 1943.B3, "The Novels of Henry Adams."
Pp. 226-50: reprints 1952.B3, "The Harmony of True Liberalism: Henry Adams' *Mont-Saint-Michel and Chartres*."

5 GRIBBEN, JOHN L. "Henry Adams: Educator." *The Serif*, 4 (June), 5-14.
In all of his writings Adams sought to urge "education for moral [later, aesthetic] power."

6 GUTTMANN, ALLEN. *The Conservative Tradition in America*. New York: Oxford University Press, pp. 125-35.
As "Conservative Manqué" Henry Adams never became an authentic "Conservative" because he "looked back and saw

only discontinuity." Relies on the *Education* to document pessimism of the "Liberal stripped of illusion."

7 HOFFMAN, FREDERICK J. *The Imagination's New Beginning: Theology and Modern Literature*. Indiana: Notre Dame University Press, passim.

"Nostalgia and Christian Interpretation: Henry Adams and William Faulkner" stresses kinship of two observers and critics of American Culture, with attention to Adams's "rebellious irritation with Puritanism."

8 JONES, HOWARD MUMFORD. *Belief and Disbelief in American Literature*. Chicago and London: University of Chicago Press, pp. 114-15.

Brief assessment of Henry Adams's acceptance of "cosmic pessimism" in the age of Mark Twain.

9 KRONENBERGER, LOUIS. "The Letters--and Life--of Henry Adams." *Atlantic*, 119 (April), 80-89.

General appreciation of Henry Adams as a writer. Reprinted: 1969.B6.

10 MANE, ROBERT. "Henry Adams." *Etudes anglaises*, 20:29-37.

Reviews Samuels's *Major Phase*, with special attention to *Chartres* and the *Education*. Also cites opinions of other critics.

11 MARTIN, JAY. *Harvests of Change: American Literature, 1865-1914*. Englewood Cliffs, New Jersey: Prentice Hall, Inc., pp. 296-309.

Surveys Adams's works while tracing his opinions as a "spokesman" of "alienation," parallel to Twain. Both were "conscious of the push of history against human ideals."

12 MONCHOUX, ANDRE. "Propos inedits sur la France dans les lettres de Henry Adams." *Revue de Littérature Comparée*, 41 (April-June), 238-74.

Relies on unpublished letters to document general statements concerning Adams's mixed response.

13 SAMUELS, ERNEST. "Introduction" to *History of the United States During the Administrations of Jefferson and Madison*. Abridged and edited by Ernest Samuels. Chicago: University of Chicago Press, pp. vi-xx.

A short account of Henry Adams's life and of the conditions surrounding the writing and publication of the *History*. Special attention to methods of organization.

1967

14 _____. "Henry Adams and the Gossip Mills." Essays in American and English Literature Presented to Bruce Robert McElderry, Jr. Athens: Ohio University Press, pp. 59-75.
Dismisses rumors concerning Adams's relationship with Elizabeth Cameron and defends the three-volume biography against charges of evasion.

15 SHAW, PETER. "Blood is Thicker than Irony: Henry Adams' History." New England Quarterly, 40 (June), 163-87.
Adams's treatment of Jefferson and his party in the History "methodically discredited the Adams family opponents and their theories, while it vindicated" the Adamses.

16 STEIN, ROGER B. John Ruskin and Aesthetic Thought in America, 1840-1900. Cambridge, Massachusetts: Harvard University Press, pp. 209, 222-26.
Considers Henry Adams's ideas about art and life, especially the influence of Ruskin on both.

17 STEIN, WILLIAM. "The Portrait of a Lady," in Perspectives on James. Edited by William T. Stafford. New York: New York University Press, pp. 166-83.
Reprint of 1959.B11.

18 SUDERMAN, ELMER F. "Skepticism and Doubt in Late Nineteenth Century American Novels." Ball State University Forum, 8 (Winter), 63-72.
Esther "is the earliest attempt to deny God's existence in the light of evidence of evolution and comparative religion."

19 VANDERSEE, CHARLES. "Henry Adams and the Invisible Negro." South Atlantic Quarterly, 66 (Winter), 13-30.
Finds Adams's "skepticism and indifference" concerning Negroes no more racist than typical attitudes in Boston.

20 _____. "Henry Adams Behind the Scenes: Civil War Letters to Frederick W. Seward." Bulletin of the New York Public Library, 71 (April), 245-64.
Prints eleven previously unpublished letters with a biographical introduction, contrasting contents with the Education.

21 _____. "The Pursuit of Culture in Adams' Democracy." American Quarterly, 19 (Summer), 239-48.
Concentrates on first chapter of the novel to study satirical attack on "culture" and on Adams himself. "The satire in Democracy was partly self-directed."

1968

1968 A BOOKS

1 LEVENSON, J. C. The Mind and Art of Henry Adams. Stanford, California: Stanford University Press.
Reprint of 1957.A1.

1968 B SHORTER WRITINGS

1 ANDREWS, CLARENCE A. "Introduction" to Democracy. New York: Airmont, pp. 3-8.
Treats Democracy as "a comedy of manners set against a backdrop of political intrigue."

2 CHAZEAUX, JEAN et EVELYNE de. "Lettres de Henry Adams: Tahiti 1891." Revue des Deux Mondes (1 September), pp. 85-100.
French translations of letters written in English, printed with an introduction. Reprinted and expanded: 1974.B4.

3 CHRISTY, ARTHUR E. "The Sense of the Past," in The Asian Legacy and American Life. New York: Greenwood Press.
Reprint of 1945.B3.

4 CURTI, MERLE. Human Nature in American Historical Thought. Columbia: University of Missouri Press, pp. 78-92.
Henry Adams seen as "the first really great American exponent of the scientific movement in historical thought and writing," an intellectual kin to Oliver Wendell Holmes, Jr., and an advocate of "tough-minded" history, who yet used "the term human nature without adequately defining it."

5 FORD, WORTHINGTON CHAUNCEY. "Introductory Note" to A Cycle of Adams Letters. Edited by Worthington Chauncey Ford. 2 Vols. New York: Kraus Reprint Co., pp. vii-xiv.
Reprint of 1920.B3.

6 FRIEDLAENDER, MARC. "Brooks Adams en Famille." Proceedings of the Massachusetts Historical Society, 80:77-93.
Poses some unanswered questions concerning the relationship between Brooks and Henry Adams.

7 GROSS, HARVEY. "Henry Adams' Broken Neck." Centennial Review, 12 (Spring), 169-80.
Compares Adams and Nietzsche as "culture heroes" and "pseudo-men-of-action."

1968

8 HARBERT, EARL N. "Henry Adams' New England View: A Regional Angle of Vision?" Tulane Studies in English, 16:107-34.
Examines Adams's efforts to achieve historical objectivity in the History.

9 HOFSTADTER, RICHARD. The Progressive Historians: Turner, Beard, Parrington. New York: Knopf, pp. 30-35.
As a "Gilded Age" historian, Henry Adams is part of "The Background" for progressive historians; he "stands . . . alone--singular not only for the quality of his prose and the sophistication of his mind but also for the unparalleled mixture of his detachment and involvement."

10 LEVENSON, J. C. "Henry Adams and the Art of Politics." Southern Review, 4 (Winter), 50-58.
His interest in "politics as an art clarifies at once Adams's relation to twentieth-century estheticism and to his eighteenth-century political inheritance." Chief example is the Education.

11 MARTIN, JOHN S. "Henry Adams on War: The Transformation of History into Metaphor." Arizona Quarterly, 24 (Winter), 325-41.
Studies "Adams' transformation of war from a fact into a metaphor of historical change and the continuity of generations" in the History and his letters.

12 MUNFORD, HOWARD M. "Henry Adams: The Limitations of Science." Southern Review, 4 (Winter), 59-71.
Although Henry Adams "did know what he meant" when he discussed science, his aim was not "objective truth." He was finally a reformer, not a scientist.

13 REEVES, JAMES and SÉAN HALDANE. "Introduction" to Homage to Trumbull Stickney. London: Heinemann Educational Books, pp. 11-13.
Describes Mrs. Elizabeth Cameron's "affair" with Stickney and Henry Adams's jealousy.

14 RICHARDSON, ROBERT D., JR. "McLuhan, Emerson and Henry Adams." Western Humanities Review, 22 (Summer), 235-42.
Like Emerson, a "pilgrim of power," Adams also shows kinship with McLuhan's "grand intellectual" design because both use "two grand historical points of relation."

15 SAWYER, FRED C. "Chronology" and "Introduction" to Memoirs of Arii Taimai (or Tahiti) by Henry Adams. Ridgewood, New Jersey: Gregg Press.

Briefly reviews facts of composition, revision, and publication.

16 SCHEICK, WILLIAM J. "Symbolism in The Education of Henry Adams." Arizona Quarterly, 24 (Winter), 350-60.
Basing his method on St. Augustine's Confessions, Adams used "Boston" and "Quincy" as "controlling organic symbols" that determined the "structure and theme" of his book.

17 SPANGLER, GEORGE M. "The Education of Henry Adams as a Source for 'The Love Song of J. Alfred Prufrock.'" Notes and Queries, 15 (August), 295-96.
Treats the Education as a source for "ragged claws."

18 SPILLER, ROBERT. The Oblique Light. New York: Macmillan.
Reprints 1948.B4.

19 STOEHR, TAYLOR. "Tone and Voice." College English, 30 (November), 152-54.
Contrasts Henry Adams's "He" with Thoreau's "I" in Walden as narrative pronouns that help to create differences in "tone."

20 TANNER, TONY. "Henry James and Henry Adams." TriQuarterly, 11 (Winter), 91-108.
Both writers functioned as "historians of themselves," although Adams found far less self-satisfaction from his art.

21 VANDERSEE, CHARLES. "The Four Menageries of Henry Adams." Arizona Quarterly, 24 (Winter), 293-308.
"Animal images" provide a "surprisingly full revelation of Adams' important attitudes toward various people and groups of people" throughout his writings.

22 _____. "Henry Adams and 1905: Prolegomena to the Education." Journal of American Studies, 2 (October), 199-224.
Reviews the events of a key year in Adams's life (and the final chapter of the Education), when he wrote "some 110 letters" and was elected to the American Academy of Arts and Letters.

23 _____. "Henry Adams' Education of Martha Cameron: Letters, 1888-1916." Texas Studies in Literature and Language, 10 (Summer), 233-93.
Prints previously unpublished letters from Adams to Martha Cameron, 1888 to 1916, with a historical introduction.

1968

24 _____. "The Mutual Awareness of Mark Twain and Henry Adams." English Language Notes, 5 (June), 285-92.
Contrary to earlier opinions, Adams did meet Twain in "January, 1886" and afterward became a model for the "unhappiest man" in Twain's What Is Man?

25 VAN NOSTRAND, A. D. Everyman His Own Poet: Romantic Gospels in American Literature. New York: McGraw-Hill, passim.
Compares Henry Adams with Poe (Chapter 9: "The Theories of Adams and Poe") in terms of personal "metaphor" and "the dramatic persona of the author." In each case, the writer "builds a metaphor . . . and then returns incessantly . . . in order to expand and develop it."

1969 A BOOKS

1 BAYM, MAX I. The French Education of Henry Adams. New York: Kraus Reprint Co.
Reprint of 1951.A1.

2 WAGNER, VERN. The Suspension of Henry Adams: A Study of Manner and Matter. Detroit: Wayne State University Press.
Selects Henry Adams's "major formal works" (History, Chartres, the Education) to demonstrate the thesis that "decisive conclusion is exactly what Adams teaches us we cannot find" (p. 182). Treats Adams as "a great stylist," "a protestant in the fullest sense," and a "genuine" humorist, who addressed himself to expressing "the deepest American truth." Special attention to literary techniques.

1969 B SHORTER WRITINGS

1 ALLEN, WALTER. The Urgent West: An Introduction to the Idea of the United States. London: John Baker, pp. 225-30.
Cites Democracy and History as evidence to show the attitudes of an earlier American elite, toward government, geographical expansion, national "progress," and popular manners and customs, in contrast to the views of other contemporary and more recent observers.

2 GUTTMANN, ALLEN. "The Education of Henry Adams," in Landmarks in American Writing. Edited by Hennig Cohen. New York: Basic Books, pp. 252-60.
Originally prepared as a lecture for a Voice of America broadcast, this brief review warns: "The Education of Henry Adams is an eccentric book because it is the order

that a strange and wonderful man made out of his own life and times."

3 HICKS, GRANVILLE. The Great Tradition. Chicago: Quadrangle Books.

Reprint of 1933.B1, with new "Foreword" and "Afterword" to explain Hicks's change in attitude. "By 1933, I had come to believe that what Henry Adams regarded as the breakdown of American civilization was really the decline of the Adams family. . . . I still think Adams was a strange combination of prophet and crybaby" (pp. 314-15).

4 HIRSCHFELD, CHARLES. "Introduction" to The Degradation of the Democratic Dogma. New York: Harper Torchbooks, pp. xi-xxvii.

Considers the relationship of the two brothers, Brooks and Henry Adams, as well as the value of their ideas in the context of modern criticism. Reprint of 1919.B1.

5 KAZIN, ALFRED. "History and Henry Adams." (Parts I and II). New York Review of Books (23 October and 6 November), pp. 24-31, 42-46.

The History shows us "the writer who, within the discipline of scholarship, has more than any other created our image of history, who in fact shapes our idea of history."

6 KRONENBERGER, LOUIS. The Polished Surface: Essays in the Literature of Worldliness. New York: Knopf, passim.

Reprints 1967.B9.

7 LANGDON, ROBERT. "A View on Arii Taimai's Memoirs." Journal of Pacific History, 4 (1969), 162-65.

Reviews the circumstances surrounding the composition of the Memoirs of Marau Taaroa, Last Queen of Tahiti (1893), "one of the few sources of information on pre-Christian society in Tahiti." An editorial note (p. 165) describes the locations of three known copies of the book.

8 LEVENSON, J. C. "Henry Adams," in Pastmasters: Some Essays on American Historians. Edited by Marcus Cunliffe and Robin W. Winks. New York: Harper and Row, pp. 39-73.

Considers Henry Adams's career as a teacher and writer of history, stressing the professionalism of his commitment, which helped to guarantee his intellectual growth. To fully understand Adams, we must seek to recover "the sense of democratic nationalism" in which he deeply believed. Special attention to Adams's editorship of the North American Review.

1969

9 MELDRUM, RONALD M. "The Epistolary Concerns of Henry Adams." _Research Studies: A Quarterly Publication of Washington State University_, 37 (September), 227-34.
Treats Adams's letters as "a highly subjective account of the same problems and interests with which Adams is concerned in the _Education_."

10 MINTER, DAVID L. _The Interpreted Design as a Structural Principle in American Prose_. New Haven: Yale University Press, pp. 103-33 and passim.
The _Education_ represents Adams's "deliberate appropriation of autobiography as a literary form" (p. 103). Its author acts as both "orderer" and "interpreter" of the subject's "failure." The book "is concerned with truth, not with fact, with poetry, not with history" (p. 105).

11 RODRIGUES, EUSEBIO L. "Out of Season for Nirvana: Henry Adams and Buddhism," in _Indian Essays in American Literature: Papers in Honor of Robert E. Spiller_. Edited by Sujit Mukherjee and D. V. K. Raghavachary. Bombay: Popular Prakashan, pp. 179-94.
Adams's interest in the Orient represented an attempt to solve the conflict between religious faith and modern science. He "never did surrender himself completely to Buddhism," although his poem "Buddha and Brahma" shows how deeply he was influenced.

12 SHAW, PETER. "The Success of Henry Adams." _Yale Review_, 50 (Autumn), 71-78.
Adams's "personal apologia" in the _Education_ still affirms "that the exceptional man could beneficently influence history," and that, "like his ancestors, he was such a man."

13 VANDERSEE, CHARLES. "Henry Adams (1838-1918)." _American Literary Realism, 1870-1910_, 2 (Summer), 89-120.
Bibliographical review of the last 20 years of scholarship under various headings: "History of Criticism," "Bibliography," "Published Manuscript Material," "Manuscript Collections," "Recent Shorter Criticism," "Work in Progress," "Areas Needing Further Attention." Subdivided and indexed. Continued in 1975.B6.

14 WASSER, HENRY. "_The Education of Henry Adams_ Fifty Years After." _Midcontinent American Studies Journal_, 10 (Spring), 85-87.
Finds scholars "still troubled by the problem of how to explain his [Adams's] mind." Suggests that a key may be found in Adams's special sense of "failure."

15 WHITE, LYNN, JR. Machina Ex Deo: Essays in the Dynamism of Western Culture. Cambridge, Massachusetts: M.I.T. Press, pp. 57-73.
Reprints 1958.B9.

1970 A BOOKS

1 CONDER, JOHN J. A Formula of His Own: Henry Adams's Literary Experiment. Chicago and London: University of Chicago Press.
Treats Chartres and the Education as "a single unit of art," which must be read with a full understanding of their author's changing attitudes toward historical determinism. "The determinist could convince only as the artist persuades, creating fictional forms with their own internal necessity."

2 LYON, MELVIN. Symbol and Idea in Henry Adams. Lincoln: University of Nebraska Press.
Detailed explications of six works, together with "eight or nine primary aspects" of Adams's thought. Studies form, "imaginative symbolism," characterization, intention, and various other literary techniques used throughout Adams's career. The comprehensive investigation of "meaning" is furthered by some forty pages of critical notes.

3 SCHEYER, ERNST. The Circle of Henry Adams: Art and Artists. Detroit: Wayne State University Press.
An expansion of five earlier articles. Perspective of the art historian reveals Henry Adams's "interest in the visual arts" as well as the aesthetic elements of Esther, Chartres, and the Education. Consideration of Adams's artistic friends and art movements of his period.

1970 B SHORTER WRITINGS

1 AUCHINCLOSS, LOUIS. "In Search of Innocence." American Heritage, 21 (June), 28-33.
Account of Adams's 1890 journey with John La Farge to Hawaii, Samoa, and Tahiti. Illustrated with watercolors by both men.

2 ______. "'Never leave me, never leave me.'" American Heritage, 21 (February), 20-22, 69-70.
Considers Henry Adams's last years (1913-1918), based on interviews with Aileen Tone, the "secretary-companion and adopted niece." See 1974.B2.

1970

3 BERCOVITCH, SACVAN. "Horologicals to Chronometricals: The Rhetoric of the Jeremiad." Literary Monographs, 3:1-124.
Traces the legacy of the Jeremiad to Adams; the Education is "the darkest outgrowth of the jeremiad tradition" (p. 94).

4 CHANDLER, ALICE. A Dream of Order: The Medieval Ideal in Nineteenth-Century English Literature. Lincoln: University of Nebraska Press, pp. 231-48.
The "failure" of Adams's medieval "vision" shows itself in Chartres, "the culminating work of the medieval revival." Surveys Adams's thought and writings about medieval life.

5 GIDLEY, M. "One Continuous Force: Notes on Faulkner's Extra-Literary Reading." Mississippi Quarterly, 23 (Summer), 299-314.
Treats the influence of the Education, especially Adams's concern with "dynamism" and "force," on Faulkner.

6 KEGEL, PAUL L. "Henry Adams and Mark Twain: Two Views of Medievalism." Mark Twain Journal, 15 (Winter), 11-21.
Contrasts Chartres with Twain's Prince and the Pauper and Connecticut Yankee to show that Adams "glorifies the middle ages," while Twain "derides the middle ages at every opportunity."

7 TATE, ALLEN. The Fathers. Chicago: Swallow Press.
Reprint of 1938.B4.

8 WASSER, HENRY. "Science and Religion in Henry Adams' Esther." The Markham Review, 2 (May), 4-6.
In Esther Adams accepted scientific evolution, but his "determinism . . . was not rigid." Both religion and science assumed unverifiable "super-sensual truths."

1971 A BOOKS

1 MANE, ROBERT. Henry Adams on the Road to Chartres. Cambridge, Massachusetts: Harvard University Press.
Studies Adams's intellectual and artistic development up to Chartres, the "prose poem" which is "undoubtedly Adams's greatest work" and which must be read as an "allegory." The real "unity" of Chartres is in the author's play of "imagination." Finally, the book is an "affirmation of Art."

1971 B SHORTER WRITINGS

1 COX, HARVEY. "The Virgin and the Dynamo Revisited: An Essay on the Symbolism of Technology." Soundings, 54 (Summer), 125-46.

Religious symbolism, such as that conceived by Henry Adams, may well have a place in the proper understanding of modern technology.

2 COX, JAMES M. "Autobiography and America." The Virginia Quarterly Review, 47 (Spring), 252-77.
Fits the Education into a tradition of American autobiography; "the new Adams is literally educating the old." Reprinted: 1971.B3.

3 ______. "Autobiography and America," in Aspects of Narrative. Edited by J. Hillis Miller. New York and London: Columbia University Press, pp. 141-72.
Reprints 1971.B2.

4 DOWNS, ROBERT BINGHAM. Famous American Books. New York: McGraw Hill, pp. 234-39.
Treats the Education as an essay in "Explaining the Universe." Adams "wrote 500 pages called Education and never defined the word."

5 GROSS, HARVEY. "Henry Adams," in The Contrived Corridor: History and Fatality in Modern Literature. Ann Arbor: University of Michigan Press.
Indebted to 1958.B3 and 1966.B8. Chapter II, "Henry Adams," focuses on the "persona" of a "blackly humorous observer," the "witness and victim" of history. Examines influences of Nietzsche and others.

6 HARBERT, EARL N. "Henry Adams," in Fifteen American Authors Before 1900: Bibliographical Essays on Research and Criticism. Edited by Robert A. Rees and Earl N. Harbert. Madison: University of Wisconsin Press, pp. 3-36.
Surveys bibliography, editions, manuscripts and letters, biography, and criticism. Special attention to the influence of the Adams family and to changes in critical interest. Reprinted: 1974.B8.

7 HARRELL, DON W. "Counterpoint in the Fiction of Henry Adams." Journal of the American Studies Association of Texas (March), pp. 71-77.
Democracy and Esther are structured to fit a pattern of "counterpoint" which their author used to set down "social and esthetic history."

1971

8 JONES, HOWARD MUMFORD. *The Age of Energy: Varieties of American Experience 1865-1915.* New York: Viking Press, passim.

The *Education* expresses "a tension between unity and multiplicity," which represents the "central doctrine" of the 1865-1915 period (p. xiii).

9 KUNKEL, FRANCIS. "Two Superfluous Men: Henry Adams and Albert Jay Nock." *Greyfriar*, 12:12-28.

Compares *Memoirs of a Superfluous Man* (1943) with the *Education*. Both writers show: "hostility to modern times," "belief in elitist education," distrust of "mass-men," concern for "the plight of women in twentieth-century America," anti-Semitism, skepticism, "naive oversimplification," "craving for personal power," fear of women, "catastrophe mentalities," among other qualities.

10 MULLER, HERBERT J. *In Pursuit of Relevance.* Bloomington/London: Indiana University Press, pp. 197-207.

Attempts to define the educative values of the *Education* (and *Chartres*) for students of today. "Most of Adams's critique of American democracy remains valid." The *Education* "is a first-hand survey by a first-rate mind, of the revolutionary era that he lived through, and that he foresaw was producing the kind of world the youth would have to live in."

11 MUNFORD, HOWARD M. "Thayer, Ford, Goodspeed's and Middlebury: A Missing Copy of *The Education of Henry Adams* Found." *Proceedings of the Massachusetts Historical Society*, 5:148-53.

Records annotations in one of Adams's personal copies of the *Education*.

12 RULE, HENRY B. "Henry Adams' Satire on Human Intelligence: Its Method and Purpose." *Centennial Review*, 15 (Fall), 430-44.

" . . . the *Education* emphasizes the almost insurmountable difficulties that confront man in his effort to understand his surroundings," and the success of its ironic method make it "one of the nineteenth century's greatest books of satire."

13 SCHMITZ, NEIL. "The Difficult Art of American Political Fiction: Henry Adams' *Democracy* as Tragical Satire." *Western Humanities Review*, 25 (Spring), 147-61.

Views *Democracy* as Henry Adams's reworking of John Quincy Adams's political feud with Andrew Jackson. Yet it is "the only political novel in the nineteenth century that succeeds as a novel. . . ."

14 TANNER, TONY. City of Words: American Fiction 1950-1970. New York: Harper and Row, passim.
Relies on the Education to show the "application of the law of entropy to society and human history," a theme popular with more recent writers such as Pynchon, Bellow, and Mailer.

15 VANDERSEE, CHARLES. "Henry Adams and the Atlantic: Pattern for a Career." Papers on Language and Literature (Fall), pp. 351-373.
Although Adams never published in the Atlantic, "between 1858 and 1861" he wrote "three long pieces" which were intended for its pages. The relationship traced here is a part of "the uniqueness of Henry Adams's literary career," his "complex ambivalence toward the literary trade."

16 _____. "The Hamlet in Henry Adams." Shakespeare Survey, no. 24, pp. 87-104.
Comparison of Adams as he appears in his writings (especially the Education) with Hamlet, to explain the common references to Hamlet made by Adams's critics.

1972 A BOOKS - NONE

1972 B SHORTER WRITINGS

1 BARBER, DAVID S. "Henry Adams' Esther: The Nature of Individuality and Immorality." New England Quarterly, 45 (June), 227-40.
Adams's ideas about individuality and immortality formed a set of incompatible principles, which help to establish the conflict in the novel and also to guarantee its "failure" as a work of art.

2 DOENCKE, JUSTUS D. "Myths, Machines and Markets: The Columbian Exposition of 1893." Journal of Popular Culture, 6 (Winter), 535-49.
Catalogues comments about the Chicago World's Fair from the Education.

3 LOEWENBERG, BERT JAMES. American History in American Thought. New York: Simon and Schuster, pp. 520-45, passim.
As "a study in paradox" (especially in History and the Education) Adams "employed irony with premeditated sharpness

so that what he actually said evoked what was deliberately left unsaid." A "determinist" in philosophy, he wrote "to explain Henry Adams to himself" but also "to instruct others."

4 MILLER, ROSS. "Autobiography as Fact and Fiction: Franklin, Adams, Malcolm X." Centennial Review, 16 (Summer), 221-32.
Uses the Education to help establish a theory of autobiography.

5 SKLAR, ROBERT. "Henry Adams and Democratic Society." Kyushu Amerika. Bungaku (Kyushu American Literature Society), 14:30-33.
Reviews Adams's career as a writer, showing how "the themes of 'The Great Secession Winter of 1860-61,' written when Adams was twenty-three years old, reappear again and again in his works of the following quarter century." Finally, "It was the History that raised the themes of democratic society and politics to the level, in Adams' words, of a 'scientific study of national character.' Adams created an epic narrative out of the tension between democratic idealism and American reality."

6 TUTOROW, NORMAN E. "A Bibliographical Appraisal of Henry Adams' Scientism." Social Sciences, 63 (February), 58-64.
A brief review of major writings stressing Adams's skill as a historian.

1973 A BOOKS - NONE

1973 B SHORTER WRITINGS

1 AARON, DANIEL. The Unwritten War: American Writers and the Civil War. New York: Knopf, Chapter 6 (p. 93f) and passim.
Henry Adams "never agonized over the human costs of the War as Whitman did or pondered like Melville its tragic import." His "discomfort" was "the story of his class."

2 BELL, DANIEL. The Coming of the Post-Industrial Society: A Venture in Social Forecasting. New York: Basic Books, esp. pp. 168-70.
Cites the History, Education, and "Rule of Phase Applied to History" to prove that Henry Adams was one of the first who "caught a sense of the quickening change of pace that drives all our lives."

1973

3 CROWLEY, JOHN W. "The Suicide of the Artist: Henry Adams' *Life of George Cabbot Lodge*." *New England Quarterly* (June), pp. 189-204.
"This study traces the genesis of *The Life of Lodge* and analyzes its thematic relationship to *The Education of Henry Adams* and Adams' late essays on the Dynamic Theory of History."

4 LEVY, ROBERT I. *Tahitians: Mind and Experience in the Society Islands*. Chicago and London: University of Chicago Press, passim.
Reports Adams's observations recorded in letters and in *Memoirs of Marau Taaroa*.

5 LINNEY, ROMULUS. *The Love Suicide at Schofield Barracks* and *Democracy and Esther* (two plays). New York: Harcourt Brace Jovanovich, pp. 111-206.
Dramatic treatment of Henry Adams's novels.

6 PERSONS, STOW. *The Decline of American Gentility*. New York: Columbia University Press, pp. 203-18.
Concentrates on *History* to prove that Henry Adams was "Tocqueville's most distinguished American disciple." Adams used irony as a weapon, in part because he was "reluctant to give up the ideal of a talented and influential gentry elite." Thus, "the mainstream of American historical thought . . . bypassed him."

7 POWNALL, DAVID E. *Articles on Twentieth Century Literature: An Annotated Bibliography 1954 to 1970*. New York: Kraus-Thomson Organization Ltd., pp. 5-16.
"An expanded cumulation of 'Current Bibliography'" in *Twentieth Century Literature*.

8 SAMUELS, ERNEST. "Introduction" to *The Education of Henry Adams*. Edited by Ernest Samuels. Boston: Houghton Mifflin, pp. vii-xx.
This edition is the first which makes use of Adams's annotations and corrections. *See also* "Textual Note" (xxi-xxv), "Appendix A" ("Excerpts from Letters of Henry Adams," pp. 507-18), "Appendix B" ("Tables," pp. 519-35), and "Notes" (pp. 539-688).

9 SHAW, PETER. "The War of 1812 Could Not Take Place: Henry Adams's *History*." *Yale Review*, 62 (Summer), 544-56.
The *History* remains "our one classic history written like those of antiquity, by an interested party." It

defends John and John Quincy Adams and indirectly attacks Jefferson and Madison.

1974 A BOOKS

1 MURRAY, JAMES G. Henry Adams. New York: Twayne Publishers Inc., Twayne's World Leaders Series.

Seven chapters arranged in three parts: "Triangulation," "Transcendentalism," "Existentialism." Printed with "Epilogue," "Notes and References," "Selected Bibliography," and "Index." Attempts "a comprehensive reading of Adams," based upon a study of his "artistic instruments," such as "Ironic Exaggeration," "Dramatic Contrast," "Image-making," and "the theme of failure."

1974 B SHORTER WRITINGS

1 ARMSTRONG, WILLIAM M., ed. The Gilded Age Letters of E. L. Godkin. Albany, New York: State University of New York Press.

Sidelights on Henry Adams's involvement with Godkin, the Nation, the North American Review, Democracy, and on Charles Francis Adams, Jr., who reviewed Gallatin for the Nation.

2 AUCHINCLOSS, LOUIS. "Aileen Tone and Henry Adams." Final chapter in A Writer's Capital. Minneapolis: University of Minnesota Press, pp. 143-54.

Explains how Auchincloss made use of Miss Tone's memories of the final years of Henry Adams's life. See 1970.B2.

3 BOYD, JULIAN P. "Jefferson's Expression of the American Mind." Virginia Quarterly Review, 50 (Autumn), 538-62.

In the History Henry Adams was "misled" into a false portrayal of Jefferson: "Adams deliberately chose the image of an artist painting a portrait, the shifting and uncertain shadows being caused not by a failure of light or of the artist's vision, but by the shifting, unsteady posture of the subject."

4 CHAZEAUX, EVELYN DE. "Introduction" to Henry Adams: Lettres des Mers du Sud: Hawaii, Samoa, Tahiti, Fidji: 1890-1891, pp. vii-xxx.

This French edition, "translated from the American," edited and annotated by Chazeaux, brings together the texts of Adams's letters and maps, photographs, and watercolor reproductions. Brief treatment of Adams's life during this period. Includes material in 1968.B2.

5 CHURCH, ROBERT L. "Economists as Experts: The Rise of the Academic Profession in the United States, 1870-1920," in The University in Society, Vol. 2. Edited by Lawrence Stone. Princeton: Princeton University Press, 571-609.

Weighs academic influence of Henry Adams (pp. 578f). Adams "aimed at reforming the society by calling the elite to their responsibilities."

6 DONOGHUE, DENIS. "The American Style of Failure." Sewanee Review, 82 (Summer), 407-32.

Adams's view of "failure" as "a fault in the system" compared with views of other writers, including Henry James, Tate, Veblen, and Trilling. Their differences show up in the contrasting styles of their work.

7 HARBERT, EARL N. "The Education of Henry Adams: The Confessional Mode as Heuristic Experiment." Journal of Narrative Technique, 4 (January), 3-18.

The Education is an example of a sophisticated art, which intends to be at once experimental and didactic. Its author was attempting to encourage some response from the reader, who holds the key to the final success of the book.

8 ______. "Henry Adams," in Fifteen American Authors Before 1900: Bibliographical Essays on Research and Criticism. Edited by Robert A. Rees and Earl N. Harbert. Madison: University of Wisconsin Press, pp. 3-36.

Reprint of 1971.B6, with minor corrections.

9 HENDERSON, HARRY B., III. Versions of the Past: Imagination in American Fiction. New York: Oxford University Press, passim.

Identifies a "new twentieth-century emphasis, first apparent in . . . Democracy, on history evolving through the present and shaping the future" ("Preface," p. xvi). Adams's "progressive imagination" worked to defeat the older forms of "holist imagination" and to "redeem history from antiquarianism," in Chartres and the Education (p. 42).

10 MILLER, ROSS LINCOLN. "Henry Adams: Making It Over Again." Centennial Review, 18 (Summer), 288-305.

"What have been described as the three major intellectual periods of Adams's life can also be identified as stages of consciousness." The Education is a "testament to his

1974

search" for "the new social scientist" who could write "new history" in the language of science.

11 MONTEIRO, GEORGE. "The Education of Ernest Hemingway." Journal of American Studies, 8 (April), 91-99.
Hemingway's work, "in certain basic characteristics . . . is what it is because of The Education of Henry Adams."

12 ROSS, RALPH. "Introduction" to Makers of American Thought: An Introduction to Seven American Writers. Edited by Ralph Ross. Minneapolis: University of Minnesota Press, pp. 3-12.
Attempts to fit Henry Adams into the intellectual history of his period. First chapter (pp. 13-48) reprints Louis Auchincloss's AWS pamphlet on Henry Adams. Contains a Selected Bibliography (pp. 265-66).

13 SHKLAR, JUDITH N. "The Education of Henry Adams by Henry Adams." Daedalus, 103 (Winter), 59-66.
"Henry Adams certainly set out to write a public autobiography." Yet, "the result is a matchless contribution to the literature of pure sadness."

14 SISSON, DANIEL. The American Revolution of 1800. New York: Knopf, pp. 3-6, 24, 409n.
Takes issue with Henry Adams's interpretation of Jefferson and the events of 1800 in the History. Describes the History as, "the archetypal work in American history upon which all other works were to be modeled."

15 STARK, CRUCE. "The Historical Irrelevance of Heroes: Henry Adams's Andrew Jackson." American Literature, 46 (May), 170-81.
Adams's "intentions of objectivity" in the History "proved no match for the temptations both to literary craft and craftiness," especially where Andrew Jackson figured in the narrative.

16 TAYLOR, GORDON O. "Of Adams and Aquarius." American Literature, 46 (March), 68-82.
Adams's Education and Norman Mailer's The Armies of the Night and Of A Fire On the Moon share "affinities." Both authors seek to "recast" history as a narrative of personal experience.

17 VITZTHUM, RICHARD C. The American Compromise: Theme and Method in the Histories of Bancroft, Parkman, and Adams. Norman: University of Oklahoma Press, passim.

Expands sections of 1965.B17. Studies influences, sources, and method of History, in comparison with works of Bancroft and Parkman, who, with Adams, express "the basic moral theme . . . --that extremes are dangerous and that social and political well-being lies in the center" (p. 208).

1975 A BOOKS - NONE

1975 B SHORTER WRITINGS

1 EPPARD, PHILIP B. "Frances Snow Compton Exposed: William Roscoe Thayer on Henry Adams as a Novelist." Resources For American Literary Study, 4 (Spring), 81-94.
Describes the circumstances surrounding the composition and appearance of Thayer's article in the Boston Evening Transcript for August 10, 1918, which named Adams as author of Democracy and Esther.

2 HAYNE, BARRIE and KATHERINE MORRISON. "Henry Adams." American Literary Realism, 8 (Summer), 180-88.
Discusses unpublished Ph.D. dissertations that consider Henry Adams, finding "very high" quality work. See also 1975.B6.

3 SCHINTO, JEANNE M. "The Autobiographies of Mark Twain and Henry Adams: Life Studies in Despair." Mark Twain Journal, 17 (Summer), 5-7.
The Education and the never-completed Autobiography of Mark Twain both express "despair" about the "diffusion of [national] interests," while showing "nostalgia for the lost era of the frontier" and a "common distrust of those who wield power."

4 SMITH, WILLIAM ANDER. "Henry Adams, Alexander Hamilton, and the American People as a 'Great Beast.'" New England Quarterly, 48 (June), 216-30.
Hamilton's famous comment, "Your people is a great beast," is traced to Adams's History but not to Hamilton himself. Adams intended "to reveal the character of the actor in his own words" but Hamilton had died in 1804 and Adams probably borrowed the quotation from the Memoirs of Theophilus Parsons (1859).

5 STARK, CRUCE. "The Development of a Historical Stance: The Civil War Correspondence of Henry and Charles Francis Adams." CLIO, 4 (June), 383-97.

Relies on letters among the Adams brothers to trace the course of Henry's "historical career" and to show that he developed literary "detachment" as a defense against subjectivity and introspection. After writing the History, Adams went on to Chartres and the Education where he attained larger subjectivity and increased personal revelation.

6 VANDERSEE, CHARLES. "Henry Adams (1838-1918)." American Literary Realism, 8 (Winter), 18-34.

Continues Vandersee's bibliographical survey (1969.B13) and includes notes on "Popularization," "Recent Books," "Bibliography," "Manuscripts and Letters," "Shorter Criticism," and some discussion of dissertations.

Index

Index

INDEX